STILL A PFC: A COMBAT MARINE IN WORLD WAR II

The Pacific Theater (1942-1945): Guadalcanal, Bougainville, Guam, & Iwo Jima

EUGENE H. PETERSON

www.stillapfc.com

First Printing May 21, 2000

Second Printing August 7, 2000

Third Printing May 18, 2011

Fourth Printing December 15, 2018

Revised April 15, 2001

Revised May 15, 2005

Revised October 2008

Revised August 2010

Revised Posthumously December 2018

ISBN: 978-0-578-42028-7

Private First Class, Eugene H. Peterson (#425802)
United States Marine Corps

CONTENTS

DEDICATION

I write this account of my life in the United States
Marine Corps at the request of my wonderful wife of 50
years, Margaret B. Peterson. I dedicate this to her for the
wonderful 50 years she has dedicated to me.

Margaret B. Peterson and PFC Eugene H Peterson

ACKNOWLEDGMENTS

Elaine Day, for her administrative assistance and patience

Fellow Marines who have shared these experiences with me.

My sons Tim and Mark and my daughter Margaret Ann, who have encouraged me in this effort.

Don Martin, my dear son-in-law, whose studies in genealogy inspired me.

PROLOGUE

WHY "STILL A P.F.C."

For years, my wife, Margaret, had asked me to put into writing my experiences in World War II. She contended our children would enjoy knowing about this part of my life. I agreed; however, my early good intention were offset by procrastination and perhaps a lack of desire on my part. Then Don Martin joined in.

My son-in-law, Donald Martin, has authored two books on his family ancestry. Don added weight to Margaret's request, when he told of his frustration over lack of information on his relative's activities in the Civil and Revolutionary Wars.

Don stated in his search for family history, certain relatives were cited as a "Private" or a "Captain" in the wars but no mention of what they did or where they fought.

The best he could hope to find was the mention of a regiment or company.

With Margaret's insistence and Don's reasoning, I finally took up the challenge. As I began this effort, I was certain I'd complete it in a couple of days in 10 or 15 pages.

I first thought I'd start with my first combat landing at Bougainville. Then good sense prevailed and I decided to begin at my induction into the Marines and move geographically and chronologically through the many ports and posts provided me. I must admit the excitement mounted. I renewed old friendships and experiences as I wrote of them.

I decided not to get mired in the horrors or waste of war. Tomes have been devoted to this subject. I chose instead to tell of my life as a Private, a grunt if you will, and how this life impacted on me.

Some sage observed, "They also serve who stand and wait." Undoubtedly true, but I distinguish between those who experience deadly combat and the others. A combat soldier, sailor, airman or Marine is different and has served under conditions that mark them forever, as brothers in arms.

I have often been asked, "How did you cope with death as an everyday fact?" I tell of losing eight buddies on one day on Guam. We acknowledged the loss then moved on. "What is past is past." We did not dwell on one or multiple losses. We simply moved on. Yesterday was an age away, this is today, we hope to see tomorrow. Perhaps cruel, but it retained our sanity. Those who stand and wait have not shared this burden.

After the war, we didn't talk much about our wartime experiences. So many had shared similar in-service events. To burden people with "War Stories" was considered boorish. Also, there were many who could not bear to recall the horror they had observed. The end result was very little retelling of one's life in the armed forces.

I am proud of having served as a Combat Marine and proud of those who served with me.

THE THIRD MARINE DIVISION - ODYSSEY

Auckland, New Zealand - January 1943
Guadalcanal - June 1943
Bougainville - 1 November 1943
Guam - 21 July 1944
Iwo Jima - 19 February 1945
Guam - 28 December 1945
Camp Gifu - August 1953
Okinawa - February 1956
Vietnam - March 1965
Desert Storm - January 1991
Okinawa - Force in Readiness - Present, as of 2010

ONCE A MARINE, ALWAYS A MARINE!

By choice, chance and God's hand, I survived some extremely trying times in the Marine Corps during World War II.

As a telephone lineman, I had the greatest opportunity to see more of the combat area than most participants. We traveled to the right flank, left flank, up front and to the rear areas to keep our telephone lines functioning and all our artillery and infantry in constant communications.

A Japanese general stated "the American troops' ability to concentrate artillery fire on a given point was a tremendous advantage." As an artilleryman, I am proud we provided this edge. Our front line troops on numerous occasions told me our artillery barrage had "stopped the Japs cold." Our constant goal.

Lest you think I am portraying myself as some kind of hero -- let me remind you, they never asked me if I wanted to go on these combat landings.

I was not a hero, but I walked among heroes.

ABOUT MY ADVERSARY

My adversary -- The Japanese Soldier.

Initially we were all swept up in the hate generated by the "sneak" attack on Pearl Harbor.

In confronting the Japanese soldier, I found it difficult to hate this man. He was courageous and crafty. He served his Emperor and nation to his death. It is hard to detest a man willing to die for his cause.

The Japanese soldier's willingness to die was at once courageous and also could be carried to a fault. The soldiers often times preferred death to fighting.

As we broke out of our Asian perimeter on Guam, I passed five dead Japanese soldiers who had committed suicide by placing a hand grenade against their chests. They were shoulder to shoulder on an embankment along the road. It was obvious the five had reached an agreement to take the easy way out. Had the five opted to fight, they could have taken some toll on our forces.

Another example of the Japanese not giving their all to carry the battle to us was to be found in the hills surrounding our landing area at Asan Beach, Guam. In a cave overlooking our landing beach, I observed a twin mounted 37mm or 40mm gun capable of rapid fire. Had a Japanese soldier or two manned these excellent weapons, they could have decimated our landing craft and troops on the beach. Our offshore Navy would have eventually silenced these guns, but for its short life it would have created havoc on the incoming Marines.

It seemed to me the Japanese soldier saw only his own personal involvement in the battle with no concept of his bigger more important role in the conduct of his army's defense scheme. The Japanese soldiers would rather die in a foxhole than seek to defeat the opposing force. I have heard stories of Japanese troops shouting obscenities at our forces but always consider such stories less than likely to have occurred. The Japanese soldiers' great plus was his stealth and mastery of camouflage. This hardly fits into a shouting exhibitionist type. (The exception to this prototype was the participants in organized banzai charges.) I have met hundreds of combat Marines who claim in all their combat experiences they never saw a live Japanese soldier. A shouter is hard to hide.

When I shared this opinion with Lou Hum, he countered, "Damn it Peterson, they yelled on Iwo." I agreed, but insisted the Japanese stealth was their combat strength.

For many years, Admiral Nagumo, the man who was in command of the December 7th strike on Pearl Harbor, has been criticized for his failure to launch a second wave of attacks on this bastion. The oil storage and repair facilities at Pearl Harbor remained intact. Once more attack on these targets would have had a devastating effect on the United States' ability to mount an early reprisal, as at Midway Island. The Japanese Admiral withdrew rather than press home his advantage. Again, we see the Japanese satisfied with his role but failing to see the bigger picture.

I find this type of thinking reflected down to even the lowliest Japanese soldier. I found the machinations of the Japanese minds caused me to be puzzled on more than one occasion. Why would a Japanese tank spare my life? Why was some of their equipment excellent and other equipment plain junk? Why were Japanese observed waving swords in the modern battle scene?

Such bravado indicated the Japanese thought their strength and belief in the Bushido code of conduct offset the superior firepower of their opponent. They were wrong.

On one occasion I observed a heavy-duty trailer of the Japanese Army; all steel, tubular steel support braces, and a heavy steel tow bar attached to the main body of the trailer by a frayed rope instead of a steel bolt or welding. You must recall in the pre-war economy "Made in Japan" carried no guarantee of quality.

In a few words, the Japanese soldier often was ready to die for his Emperor but hesitant to live and press for a final victory. When he did hold fast, we experienced Tarawa, Saipan, Iwo Jima, Peleliu, and Okinawa.

In summary, the mental quirks of the Japanese mind often worked to our advantage.

REFLECTIONS OF MY MARINE EXPERIENCE

I graduated from South Shore high school in 1942. The only thought I had about my future was which branch of the armed service I would join. The war at this point was all-consuming and all my friends and fellow graduates were joining some branch of service.

I joined the Marines in July 1942. Why the Marines? My motivation was provided by a group of neighborhood boys who were joining the Marines. There was "Moon" Mahoney, Bosco Sabina, Danny Sullivan, and Joe Nottingham. All worthies from our South Shore community. Actually, I knew little about the Marines. Perhaps I should have inquired.

We were given physicals at the recruiting station in downtown Chicago. I was amazed at the number of men rejected at this point. I was even more amazed that

I passed. At six feet tall and one hundred and forty pounds, I was like a shadow among the hulks that passed.

The process moved rapidly from this point. We were told to meet at the La Salle Street train station in three days. We said goodbyes to our family and friends and we were on our way to the West Coast.

As our train stopped at depots along our route, volunteers came to the train with coffee and doughnuts. These wonderful citizens wanted to show their support for "our boys in the service."

The train ride provided time to read and write letters home. There were dice games and cards for the more adventurous. I knew little about gambling but won one hundred and forty five dollars shooting dice. I mention this because it was by far more money than I had ever had before.

Our three days train ride ended in San Diego, California.

This California metropolis afforded us our first glimpse of a city prepared for war. Chicago and the inland cities we passed through on our way to the West Coast were relatively unchanged by our entrance into this world conflict. But here in San Diego, we found this coastal city prepared for a Japanese assault.

The airplane plants and a good portion of the city were covered by miles of camouflage netting. Atop these steel nets, an entire make believe city was displayed; streets, houses, trees and lawns. This faux city would give an aerial observer the impression the city of San Diego extended almost to the Pacific shore line. Nestled under this make believe city, the Consolidated Vultee Aircraft plant and other defense plants remained hidden. A remarkable bit of legerdemain! The vast subterfuge would remain for the entire war.

Spaced around this netting and other parts of the city were anti-aircraft gun emplacements, ominously threatening the empty skies. Also massive searchlights flashed across the evening clouds. One had the impression this city was prepared to fight. The overabundance of Army, Navy, and Marine uniforms assured us the war was near.

As we were transported to the Marine Corps base, we passed under miles of the mock city mentioned above. The massive steel supports undergirding the fake city over us were impressive.

What moved us most was how seriously they were taking the Japanese threat. To our Midwest contingent, the were was newspaper stories and a smattering of movie newsreels. It was a sobering fact we were now living in a possible war zone; a reality that would be with us for the next three years.

We were bused to the Marine Corps Base. Interestingly, as we entered the base, most of the Marines paid us an inordinate amount of interest. They seemed to enjoy shouting "You'll be sorry" in a rather uniform singing manner. We were greeted by this shouting at every turn as we crossed the base to the "Recruit Depot." As we entered the Recruit Depot, a section located at the southern end of the Marine Base, there occurred a remarkable change. The administrators of this enclave were very somber and obviously unimpressed with the sacrifices we had made to join the Marines.

A short but relatively pleasant welcome was given by an officer of unspecified rank and then a particularly vicious Sergeant took charge of us.

Sergeant Nasty informed us our present status -- we were "nothing." He proclaimed enthusiastically "You are not civilians, you are certainly not Marines. You are nothing. You are a low form of animal dung (not his word) smelling up the sacred sands of the Marine Corps Base, San Diego, California."

This was hardly the reception we anticipated but better than what was to come. The perception of those shouting at our bus as we drove to the "Recruit Depot" was profound. We were sorry and had a feeling things were about to go downhill.

We were designated Platoon 602 of 1942 (this meant

601 Platoons of recruits had preceded us that year.) Our platoon's median age would be shy of 18 years. Just kids moving into a man's world.

The makeup of our Platoon 602 was half Chicagoans and half Texans. This diabolic mix was not by chance. I am certain someone in charge of making boot camp miserable had evolved this mix as a certain way to assure fights.

Up to this point in my life I probably hadn't given any serious thought to the Civil War except in a history class. I was now among individuals ready to fight to defend Robert E. Lee. Even more amazing, many of the Chicagoans found it a point of honor to uphold Ulysses S. Grant. This all came to a head when the Texas boys chose one of their own to settle the War between the States by fighting Joe Nottingham, the choice of the Chicago worthies.

As a great supporter of Joe Nottingham and Ulysses S. Grant, I found many Texans ready to take my bet. I wagered the entire $145.00 I had won shooting dice on the train. (Fortunately only a few of the Chicagoans and none of the Texans knew that Joe Nottingham was a C.Y.O boxing champion of Chicago.) Unsporting, the unseeded Texans hit Joe Nottingham with a haymaker that sent Joe into the ropes and into my arms. I slapped Joe back to life and he was up at the eighth count! Joe survived a beating in the first round. He won the next two rounds handily but Sergeant Nasty, our drill instructor (D.I.) called the fight a draw. Happily I kept my $145 and both Generals Lee and Grant came through unscathed and unbowed.

Why Texans hated Chicagoans and vice versa may be clarified in my later discussion of precombat hostility syndrome.

We were involved in the unusual "boot camp" routine. An excess of medical shots, endless marching (called romp and stomp), Sergeant Nasty in your face; real or imagined missteps bringing punishment to the entire platoon; and very short periods of recreation (called organized grab ass.)

We began to talk like Marines. The floor was the deck; the toilet was the head; walls were bulkheads; and we told time in 24-hour segments.

GOODBYE VICTOR WETTERQUIST

I asked D.I. Sergeant Nasty to let me have the afternoon off having had a tough session that morning with the base dentist.

He said I'd have to turn out after lunch because we were going to have a light day of "organized grab ass."

We were marching to the sandy area of the Marine base referred to as the "boondocks." Our rank was marched out single file. Then the front taller ranks were doubled back to face the small members of our platoon. Another unfair Marine practice. This placed me in front of a rather small Marine I knew only as Wetterquist.

The morning of dental drilling, bad noon meal and Sergeant Nasty had left me in a vicious, smoldering hate I intended to vent on this poor slob before me. We were issued boxing gloves and told to box with the man we faced. I could hardly wait for the whistle to blow so I could beat the unwary Wetterquist into oblivion. The whistle blew -- that was the last time I saw Wetterquist. This feather merchant hit me with a flurry of punches, jabs, hooks and every other hit known to man.

I covered my head, he hit my stomach. I'd cover my mid section, he pelted my face. Finally, I was saved from a punch drunk fate by the whistle.

As we returned to our camp, I asked Wetterquist where he learned to box. He said he was the state of Illinois lightweight champ. My bad luck continued. Out of the entire Platoon, I have to pick a boxing champ.

A NIGHT AT THE MOVIES

After our long day of boot camping we were marched to the base outdoor movie theater. The loudspeaker blared out popular records. The biggest responses were for the "Strip Polka," "Deep In The Heart of Texas" (by Bob

Wills) and "Don't Sit Under The Apple Tree." The the evening movie was shown to an audience half asleep. Our days took a toll.

ANOTHER LOSS

Imperceptibly subtle changes had occurred. I entered the Marines as Eugene H. Peterson. I was now Private Peterson 425802 (my serial number.) I had lost my first name. A few called "Pete" but my first name was gone for the duration of my time in the service except when I signed the payroll and my final discharge.

A GLIMMER OF HOPE

Danny Sullivan's dad was a close friend of the Commanding Officer of Navy Pier, Chicago. Danny's dad told us if we wrote this Navy Officer and requested transfer to the Navy Pier Chicago he was sure such requests would be honored. All our South Shore gang and I wrote and received acknowledgement from the Navy captain. Wow, what a break -- we would be back in Chicago learning Aviation Motor repair.

LIFE ON THE RANGE

A large part of our bootcamp was spent at Camp Matthews near San Diego. This was the rifle range where I would learn to fire my 1903 Springfield Rifle Caliber 30 serial number 384384. (They told me I'd never forget that serial number and they were apparently right.)

The accuracy of this rifle was amazing. At prone position (lying down) I could score "possible" (perfect) at 500 yards. After adjusting the sight for elevation and windage, I could hit the bullseye 10 out of 10 shots. At 500 yards the bullseye looked like a small dot. If I held the rifle tight and squeezed the trigger, the results were perfect. We fired in sitting, kneeling, prone, and standing positions. Unfortunately the day we fired "for record" my only "possible" was a prone position. I scored as a "Marksman" and not the coveted "Expert Marksman."

THE MARINE AND HIT RIFLE

The Marine Corps places a special aura around the rifle. In boot camp we were told to consider it as a wife. You pampered it and when in use you squeezed it. If you dropped your rifle—you slept with it. In my entire life in the Corps I always had a rifle that got more cleaning than I did. When needed, it functioned beautifully.

We were constantly told we may have a specialty in the Marines but we were always to remember we were riflemen first.

THE VISIT OF PRESIDENT ROOSEVELT TO THE SAN DIEGO MARINE BASE

My first impression was the Marine Base was apparently under siege. Machine guns were set up on the roofs; sentries were doubled at all of the base's entrances; flags festooned every corner of the parade ground; and troops of Marines were being assembled all along the parade area.

We stood in our ranks anticipating a life changing experience. We were told President Franklin Delano Roosevelt was coming to inspect us. I only hoped he would find my rifle up to his expectancy.

We stood at ease for over an hour then we heard the long awaited word: Attention!!

We froze as erect statues. Then, down the parade ground we heard the sound of a Ford engine. Yes, it was the President. But alas -- he was driven past, at about 5 miles an hour, smiling and waving his hat. He'll never know how I pressed my shirt, shined my shoes and awaited his approval. Another of life's cruel moments.

TO ERR IS TO VOLUNTEER

The last week of "bootcamp" I made a big mistake. I agreed to "observe" the communications school one Sunday afternoon. I took this opportunity to break up the monotony of "Recruit Depot." By this simple act of "observing" the communication school I was irretrievably locked into a life as a communications man for my entire time in the Marine Corps. Not very fair, but Marine life seldom was.

Our recruit Platoon 602 broke up. All my Chicago friends were off to Navy Pier Chicago, Illinois. I moved to the Northern end of the Marine Corps Base and Communications school.

How many times had I been told to volunteer for nothing? I hadn't really. I merely agreed to "observe." This really hurt. I never saw my Chicago friends of Platoon 602 again until after the war.

MRS. FEELEY

Before I leave the "Recruit Depot" I would like to recount one event that touched me deeply. In my sixth week of bootcamp I was designated a supernumerary and told to report to the visitors center. My job was to be a "gopher." When visitors came to the base looking for loved ones, I would go to the proper platoon or school and seek out the wanted Marine.

I hadn't been in the visitor's area very long when a very bedraggled woman carrying her shoes hobbled in. My God! That's Mrs. Feeley, Bob "Red" Feeley's mom! I approached her and when she saw me she screamed my name and broke into tears. She gushed "Gene, Gene, I've come to see Bobby. I sat up on a bus all the way from Chicago. I had to sit in the bus' aisle on my suitcase. I had to see Bobby before he went overseas." The officer in charge of the visitor's area came over to help comfort Mrs. Feeley. I went into recruit depot to fetch Bob Feeley. "Red" was as happy to see me as his mother had been. When I told him his mom had come to see him he couldn't believe she had made the trip.

The Feeley reunion was something to behold. Tears and hugs, tears and hugs. The Sergeant in charge expressed the hope that someone would care that much for him. "Red" Feeley and his mother departed for some time together. Red was hit on Guadalcanal. I saw him again in 1945.

COMMUNICATION SCHOOL

It was hard to believe bootcamp was over. Our new home was a second floor barracks at the North end of the San Diego Marine base.

We made the move on Friday afternoon and were told we were on liberty until Monday morning. After the strict confinement of bootcamp, we were stunned by this new freedom.

We all donned our wooly unpressed, green uniform, hoping we could be taken for Marines. Our near bald heads and apparently new fleecy wool uniforms marked us indelibly as neophytes (or perhaps new Privates.)

We determined the lights and streets of San Diego would be too much. Our alternative was the base beer garden, Shop Schute. Alas, we had dreamed of freedom for a couple of months but now found it too heady. After all, a few beers with the remnants of our recruit depot platoon wasn't all that bad.

At Communication School we were divided into radio men and telephone men. We were told our designation was determined by our ability to separate dots from dashed on a telegraph key. I suspect were were radio men or telephone men based on the needs of the Corps. Telephone communication was the primary mode of communication in the Marine Corps of World War II. Our radios were too iffy and could be "read" by the enemy.

As telephone men, we were taught to climb poles with steel climbers (you either had it or you didn't. I did.) We learned how to lay wire in trees, on the ground, or wherever it was required. Communicators' use of code names and procedures was hammered home.

A memorable incident occurred during one class period in telephone school. We all came to attention as an officer entered our class with a directive from Commandant Holcomb of the U.S. Marines. It read, "Anyone possessing knowledge of the Japanese language make this known to your Commanding Officer immediately." Still at attention, one hand arose from our group. At once the attending Sergeant snapped, "You speak Japanese, Grogan?" "Yeah, Sergeant, ah do." (Grogan was from Arkansas.) "Well say something, Grogan." Unmoved and very confidently Grogan spoke "Tok-kee-o!" The message-carrying officer, the Sergeant in charge and the whole class erupted in laughter. Grogan laughed the loudest.

After our seven week of bootcamp, Communications School, while not pleasant, was a step above the former. The food was better. We were served at tables of 10 Marines (no long chow lines.) We were required to stand at attention until the command "seat" was given. Under the watchful eye of our Sergeants the tall guys had to remain at attention. The shorter Marines would be unseen as they garnered all the choice items on the table. Most of the side of the mouth threats were ignored by the foraging runts. In the Marine Corps the food was seldom good, but always plentiful.

In Communications School, I met Ron Norman and Lou Hum. Our friendship lasted through the war. Ron Norman had that innate ability to always look neat and clean. I often said Ron Norman could fall in a mud puddle and come out looking better than those around him. Ron's close buddy was Lou Hum. Lou was a great guy and very generous. He was my source of free cigarettes for many months.

BARRACK ROOM HUMOR

With little else to entertain us, we often shouted "Attention" feigning the entrance of our Commanding Officer. One Saturday afternoon a few of the guys were playing poker on a barracks box between double decker bunks. As the Commanding Officer entered the barracks room I shouted "Attention." Bill McNamara, his back to the entrance, thought I was kidding and commented "Peterson, you wouldn't recognize that dull turd if he did show up." The C.O. cleared his throat knowingly. Bill McNamara stood up sharply, hit his head on the upper bunk and peed in his pants. The C.O. left without comment. Our barracks roared.

WAXING CLEVER

I was standing outside the Communications School talking to a couple of Marines when I was hailed by a Lieutenant. I approached with the required salute.

The Lieutenant had a problem. He wanted his red Chevrolet convertible Simonized. He handed me the Simonize and cloths. While he didn't order me to Simonize his car, there was a strong implication.

It took only about 15 minutes to apply the sticky Simonize to the entire car. The car was in the bright San Diego sunshine as I left the job to answer chow call. After lunch I passed the car and observed the sticky Simonize had burned its way into the paint. I strongly suspect that beautiful red car remains a dull gray red to this day. So much for misplaced authority.

FIELD MUSIC SCHOOL

Located next to Communication School was the Field Music School. Every morning the Marine Corps Base Band would form up and parade to the flagpole at the center of the base parade ground. They always played the "Marine Hymn" and "Semper Fidelis."

Then at eight o'clock sharp as the flag was raised, the band played "The National Anthem." After "colors" (word used for the morning flag raising and evening lowering of the flag) the band would return up the parade ground playing "Stars and Stripes Forever."

I always made sure I was on the parade grounds to see this daily performance.

A FINAL WORD

At the end of our Communications school, we had a

rather informal graduation session. (I hesitate to call it a ceremony.)

The old Sergeant thanked us for our efforts. Then he pointed out the difference between a telephone linesman and the rest of the Corps in combat. He bluntly stated, "While they stay in their fox holes, you will be out and about keeping your lines functioning. Not pretty, but it's your piece of the action." He then smiled and concluded, "I always save this ominous news for the last days at Communications School." There was a smattering of laughter at the Sarge's "good news."

PFC Eugene H Peterson at Camp Dunlap, California

CAMP DUNLAP AND "M" BATTERY

When Communication School ended after seven intensive weeks, we were loaded on a bus for a short trip to Camp Elliott in San Diego not far from the Marine Corps Base. We stayed at Camp Elliot for a few hours before assignment to the 12th Marines departing for Camp Dunlap, Niland, California.

At this juncture of my Marine Corps experience, I was too uninitiated to realize the lifesaving event that had taken place. I was assigned to the 12th Marines, an artillery regiment. I have never met a telephone man assigned to our infantry regiments that survived Bougainville, Guam and Iwo Jima. I was to learn one did not live long running around the front lines repairing wires. I have experienced enough frontline time to realize how short lived this could be. My fortunate placement in the 12th Marines became apparent to me in our first combat experience.

Camp Dunlap was in the California desert at the foot of the Chocolate Mountains in the southeast corner of California. Our new home proved hot in the day and bitter cold at night. A very spartan facility. We lived in tents. Our showers and toilet were unheated and we had structured mess halls.

I was assigned to "M Battery, 4th Battalion, 12th Marines, 3rd Marine Division. Our Division was very new, having been established in September 1942. This newly formed entity had a few veterans from the 10th Marines 2nd Marine Division. The Marine Corps was experiencing an unprecedented expansion. To accommodate this, some seasoned veterans from senior Divisions were sent into newly formed Divisions and regiments to teach the neophytes the ropes. Our Commanding Officer of "M" Battery was Captain William Gilliam.

The "M" Battery enlisted Chief was "Top" Warner (Top Sergeant of First Sergeant) we later referred to as "Pop" Warner. Usually a pleasant person with a streak of Marine that could be tough as nails. "You didn't cross the Top" became the mantra of the day. Private James "Stinkie" Clark would soon experience the down side of the "Top."

With me, in my new assignment, were Ron Norman and Lou Hum. New friends were coming into my life as fast as introductions could be made. There was A.B (Al) Miller, a fellow Chicagoan, C.W. Bowman, Bauerly a Cajun from New Orleans, Victor Lukas from Michigan and others with whom I was destined to go overseas.

Our training began immediately. M Battery and the other Batteries of the 4th Battalion 12th Marines were out in the desert on maneuvers almost without respite. We laid wire all over the California Desert and picked up wire all over the California Desert. We were trained as forward observers for our battery and we were able to do it. The pinpoint accuracy of our guns surprised me. The sound of "forward observer" was ominous.

There was always scuttlebutt about when and where we were going. We were certain of one thing; we were destined for the South Pacific. We didn't fret about our lack of definite word. We knew we were on a fast track and we would move as the Corps directed. There was little fear of being left behind.

We always held our liberties as something special. It was a pleasure to be away from regimentation. We could have liberty in a number of towns in the Imperial Valley of California. Unfortunately, they were all basically the same so we spent most of our time in Brawley.

PFC at CampDunlapp, California - 1942 - Note Reising Gun

THE ARRIVAL OF THE 2ND BATTALION

There were rumors our 2nd Battalion 12th Marines was coming to Camp Dunlap. It was one rumor that came to be. The 2nd Battalion, 12th Marines arrived at Camp Dunlap from the east coast. One would have thought a band of Nazi storm troopers or a Japanese suicide squad had arrived. There was immediate hostility whenever the 4th Battalion and 2nd Battalion met.

Please, I can't explain this enmity, I merely report the condition that existed. Fights would break out over nothing worth mentioning. We were experiencing what I term the Stateside Warrior Complex or precombat hostility syndrome. Perhaps it was tension produced by the unknown future; leaving home and loved ones; and an aggressive thrust in Marine training. These factors may have contributed to a hostile attitude and readiness to show one's manhood to fellow Marines.

Prior to shipping overseas, fighting seemed to be the answer to any real or imagined slight. Comparing this precombat feistiness to the post combat calm was something I enjoyed witnessing. After experiencing the shock of death dealing combat against the Japanese, I observed little or no need to prove one's manliness. Real combat meant we were no longer involved with other hostile individuals or branches of our armed services, but with our brothers in arms. In combat and after combat we loved having as many people on our side as possible. I might add after real combat, we sought peace wherever we could find it.

CAMP DUNLAP FALL OF 1942

Our training continued unabated. Just before Christmas, it was announced there would be a limited number of furloughs. Unfortunately, I was not a winner in this lottery. I spent a sad Christmas at Camp Dunlap. It was my first Christmas away from home. Al Miller and I shared a great Christmas banquet in the Camp Dunlap mess hall. Turkey with all the trimmings. Because of the recent furloughs the Camp personnel was low and I feel this added to the abundance of food at the banquet. I asked Al Miller if he had any qualms eating a "Christmas" meal. He replied being Jewish made him very ecumenical in his eating habits. We laughed over this. Al and I shared many laughs in the face of some bad circumstances over the next few years.

Al Miller and I shared a great appreciation of popular music. Our favorite recording was Bunny Berigan's "I Can't Get Started With You." On numerous occasions we would call disc jockeys to request "Can't Get Started" only to learn the record was broken, on loan, or just not available. We were never able to get our favorite record played. (Two years later as I climbed aboard a ship at Iwo Jima, Al Miller had the P.A. system play "I Can't Get Started.") Al was a beauty. Al and I often took our liberties together in Brawley. Unfortunately the town needed some places for us to be entertained. It was anticipated the announced opening of the New Moon Bar and Grill would fill this void.

THE PASSING OF THE NEW MOON BAR AND GRILL

In our Marine world, our liberty was divided into Port and Starboard watches. Half our personnel was designated Port and the other half Starboard. This meant on any given day, half our men could have liberty, shore leave, freedom to go to town unencumbered by any

Marine duties. This applied only when we were in Camp, not afield.

Unfortunately I did not have liberty on this particular night when the social event of Brawley California was the gala opening of the New Moon Bar and Grill. This event was given all the anticipated excitement such an event should elicit. The Marines on the Port watch streamed into Brawley heading, as a man, to the grand opening of the establishment. In this anxious group was E.L. "Smitty" Smith and his date of the evening, "Rosie," an itinerant tomato picker of Mexican extraction. Not exactly a beauty but neither was Smitty.

It is reported the evening shaped up as a grand affair. Party favors, balloons, paper streamers, noise makers and and opening drink on the house. After the symbolic toast to future greatness, the New Moon Bar and Grill was officially declared open and the best part of the entertainment scene of Brawley California.

It happened rather quickly, a smell of smoke, a flash of fire from the rear area, screams of fire and a wild evacuation of the bar. Alas, the New Moon Bar and Grill burned to the ground on its opening night.

In Camp Dunlap the Starboard watch was alert to possible fire fighting duty. The word quickly passed that there was a large fire in downtown Brawley. We never passed beyond the alert and after a while we were told our services would not be needed.

Our boys on the "Port watch" dragged back into Camp. They had all witnessed the fire and told us the ruin was complete. I noticed Smitty was one of the few not expressing regret over the demise of the New Moon Bar and Grill. I asked Smitty, "You don't seem to share the sorrow over the New Moon loss?" Smitty seemed hesitant but replied, "That bartender told me to 'get that spick bitch out of here and across the tracks where she belonged." I left but before going I threw a match into the waste paper basket in the head (toilet.)" Smitty cracked a broad smile and said "He didn't have to say that. I like Rosie and he really hurt her." After this confession I always paid particular attention when Smitty appeared to be getting upset.

Life in Camp Dunlap was a series of training problems (simulated combat maneuvers,) inspections, and occasionally turning out for Court Martial read offs. These public airings of Court Martial findings were very formal affairs with our entire Brawley assembled at attention to here the verdict from on high.

THE READING OFF OF PRIVATE CLARK - A COURT MARSHALL REPORT

A classic example of this process was the "reading off" of Private James Clark. Some excitement had been provided when Jim "Stinkie" Clark came back to camp slightly tipsy from strong drink. Sergeant Warner told him to "Shut up and go to bed." Stinkie's response to Sergeant Warner precipitated a Summary Court Martial. It was reported in the formal Court Martial findings that "Said Private Clark did on, November 28, 1942 say to Sergeant Warner "blow it out" or words to that effect."

Actually, Private Clark had said "Blow it out your ass." The entire Battery knew what Private Clark had said and at the read off anticipated how the report would read. Now as we stood at attention the First Sergeant read from the bland Court Martial record. When Sergeant Warner got to the charge, "Said Private Clark said to Sergeant Warner "blow it out or words to that effect." Even as I stood at attention, I noticed the rank in front of me rise perceptible as they also stifled their laughter. Justice had been served and the defendant had been misquoted.

NO ROOM FOR ERRING

Corporal Chuck Reinhart became a Private when standing inspection. After presenting his Reising Submachine gun for inspection, he pulled the trigger and discharged three or four live rounds at full automatic. This was an inexcusable act. The Marines were very aware of the danger of loaded pieces and if you erred, you paid. Extreme precaution was taken to assure against accidental discharge of weapons. Even with all these efforts in place, accidental discharge of weapons happened. Even in combat we would "load and lock" to assure there was no accidental discharge.

(Incidentally, John Wayne in all his movies never got this right. He always said "lock and load." You cannot load a locked weapon.)

ALWAYS A RIFLEMAN

I am often asked about the weapons the Marines gave to its troops.

The M1 Garand rifle was the basic arm of our infantry units. This was a marvelous rifle. It provided rapid fire of eight rounds by merely pulling the trigger. It was deadly accurate and hard hitting. It had replaced the Springfield 1903 bolt action rifle I qualified on in boot camp. The superior fire power of the M1 had another feature one could only appreciate if one had spent weeks firing the '03. The '03 Springfield kicked like a mule and it would black and blue your shoulder in a short while. The M1 had a minimum kick about one fifth of the '03. When you spent the day beating your shoulder to a pulp, you could enjoy the M1 Garand.

I was issued a Harrington & Richards-Reising submachine gun when I first joined "M" Battery. This was a classic piece of junk. I never fired it at full automatic that it did not jam after the second or third shot. We claimed we could hear it rust and it was so unbalanced it could not be used as a club.

In an effort to supply the communications with a light side arm we were eventually issued M-1 Carbines. This was an excellent rifle that fired a 30 caliber bullet and carried a clip of 20 rounds (later models held larger magazines.) We always carried two spare clips slung onto the butt of this rifle. This gave us a supply of sixty rounds in a very compact rifle. (Keep in mind we had to carry this rifle everywhere but we also had to carry telephones, wire and tools of our particular specialty, and a trenching tool - a shovel or pick.)

I enjoyed the M1 Carbine because it was easy to clean and operate. I never had a jam or misfire with this weapon. It fired as fast as you could pull the trigger.

On Iwo Jima, Harry Kelly loaned me his 45 caliber pistol but I never fired the piece. I kept it in my fox hole but carried my M1 rifle as I moved across the island.

As you can see by the above, the Marines always kept in mind we were basically riflemen, no matter our specialty.

THE "OLD CORPS"

The Marines with ten or more years in the Corps were constantly telling us tales of "the old corps." Among this group we had those dubbed "China Marines." This designated an elite group of Marines that had served in Peking, China in the "Horse" Marines. Those worthies had custom made uniforms beautifully fitted and lined with silk brocade with a large multi-colored dragon expertly worked into the fabric. What amazed me was these custom-fitted Marines had been paid twenty-one dollars a month.

The tales of China service included the employment of coolies that cleaned their barracks, shined their shoes, belts, and brass for about one dollar a month.

The tales about Eurasian and Chinese women were unbelievable and for the most part, we didn't believe them.

One of our beloved "old Marines" was Sergeant Pankavich. Ponky had been a heavyweight boxing champ in the Pacific Fleet. He was the purveyor of many wild "China Marine" yarns.

Many of these "old Marines" had served with the 4th Marine Regiment in China. They sadly reflected on the fate of the 4th Marines. As war loomed, this doomed regiment was reassigned to the Philippines where they fought valiantly until they were completely overrun by the Japanese. Few survived.

Then there were the old timers (30 and 40 years of age) who spoke of Chateau Thierry and Belleau Woods. Service in Nicaragua and aboard ships of the fleet.

These old Marines had found a home in the Marine Corps. We wartime enlistees found it hard to relate to that kind of life.

Many of our old Corps had served in the 2nd Marine Regiment affectionately referred to as the "Pogeybait (candy) Second." Seems the Second Regiment shipped out for China with two tons of candy bars and one ton of ammunition (sounds good to me.)

Some of these "old Marines" had returned to serve the Corps at the outbreak of World War II. We referred to them as "retreads." They were not considered combat ready, but did guard duty or other duty out of harm's way.

10-DAY FURLOUGH

In early January 1943, we learned another group would receive 10 day furloughs. Bingo! I was chosen as was Al Miller. We entrained for Chicago. Al was determined to marry his sweetheart Ruth Pentelliott. This was going to have to be a fast marriage ceremony because we only had ten days and 4 or 5 of these days were spent on the train. (Planes were unavailable except with government priority.) Al accepted the time constraints but said he wanted to be married before he went overseas.

My time in Chicago was all I expected it to be. My mother and father and sister Muriel insisted we have a professional photograph of the family. I had to see my girlfriend and high school chums (so many were already in the the service.)

There was a whirl of 4 or 5 days of busy stuff. Then I received a telegram from Captain Gilliam telling me to report to the Marine Corps Base, San Diego and not Camp Dunlap. This was a certain indicator we were about to ship overseas. I attempted to make light of it but my family knew what the telegram meant.

At the Chicago train station, I met Al Miller, his wife the former Miss Pentelliot and Al's family and Al's in-laws. Al had received the letter from Captain Gilliam. The elder Pentelliot grabbed me firmly and said, "Peterson, you take good care of Al and when you both come home I promise we'll have a party at the "Chez Paree" (#1 hot spot in Chicago,) the whole city of Chicago will talk about." I responded, "You have a deal." Then it was all hugs, kisses, and tears. We were off!

The train ride back to San Diego was a sad journey for

STILL A PFC: A COMBAT MARINE IN WORLD WAR II

Al. In my youthful naivete, I looked forward to moving into combat in the Pacific.

Upon arrival in "Dago" (San Diego) we were bedded down in tents on the western side of the Base's parade ground. We learned the 12th Marines had trucked down from Camp Dunlap and three Marines had been killed in a truck accident. Every time we made a major move some casualties were incurred by accidents.

Before departing "Dago", I must comment on this seamy town. Servicemen were held in low esteem, cheated, and exploited by a cold unfriendly populace. Although the armed services provided a major part of Dago's income, servicemen were fair game for any underhanded way to extract their money. Very few servicemen had a kind word for "Dago."

PACKING THE OLD ENGLISH ARMY FIELD DESK

My friend E.L. Smith (of New Moon's fire fame) and I were involved in building crates and frames for shipping desks, gun sights and other items that had to be carefully protected in transit.

Smithy was placing 2x4's around a field desk. He seemed to be having difficulty driving nails into the very hard lumber.

When out of nowhere, an irate Major grabbed Smithy's

hammer and snapped "What kind of a dumb son of a bitch can't use a hammer properly?" Smithy and I stood back as the Major proved he could wield a hammer. As he was putting on his exhibition of hammer proficiency, I felt I should have told the Major that Private Smith did not take criticism very well. As he returned the hammer to Smithy, he stated the desk being crated was his and that it was "an old English Army Field Desk used by many members of his family." He stated it had to be crated to assure it did not move while in shipment.

The Major departed as quickly as he appeared. I saw in Smithy's eyes that look I saw when he returned from the New Moon's Bar and Grill's demise.

Smithy now entered into his work as a man possessed. He kept repeating the Major's last words "not move while in shipment." He would lay a 2x4 across the "old english Army Field desk" then drive a six inch spike through the 2x4 into the mahogany top of the field desk. After applying six to eight spikes into the desktop, he administered a like number to each side and the bottom continuing his chant "no movement in shipment."

As we left for lunch, Smithy assured me the desk would not move in transit. He reveled in the fact "there are times one gets a great deal of satisfaction in a job well done."

I am certain the Major's questioning Smithy's family lineage drove Smithy's enthusiasm.

MONEY WOES

In the service, we always dreamed of getting home to friends and family. Another constant was never having any money. The only time I had any money was in the islands where there was nothing to buy. (The $145 I won on my way to bootcamp paid for my furlough home.) I found the $52 per month, less insurance and incidentals, never went very far. A private's pay was $50 a month. I received $2 extra as a Private First Class. (My cup runneth over.)

AWAKENING INDIAN

Our assigned tent area at the Marine Corps Base was not very well lit and on a rainy night with wind whipping around the nearly deserted tent area, there was created a Hollywood type spooky setting.

I was deep in thoughts about my family as I wrote them about my recent furlough. I was shocked into reality by a scream that would do any banshee proud. I leaped to the center of the tent and spun around to face the direction of the scream. Actually, it was an Indian war whoop. Barnett, a full blown Choctaw Indian, was the source of the scream. Barnett had awakened himself with his scream of the century. At this point we were both laughing. "My God, Barnett, you scared the hell out of me." Barnett replied, "I know, I scared myself." Screams such as this kept Barnett off the front lines in our combat areas (I should have thought of this.)

THE BLOEMFONTEIN

As were were to learn when time came for us to move, we moved. Buses took us to San Diego pier and we boarded a Dutch ship "The Bloemfontein." This was by far the worst ship in all the world's navies. We were stacked 6 or 8 bunks high in the hold of this floating misery. We were in this poorly ventilated hold that reeked of vomit as we began to experience sea sickness. These were our quarters for 17 days.

Before leaving San Diego, I was sitting on a hatch cover of the Bloemfontein with an elderly Sergeant talking about our pending voyage. Someone shouted "attention" and we all stood up as a general officer approached us. He singled out the elderly Sergeant and saluted him. I though at first the General had been too quick on his salute. I learned later that the elderly Sergeant had been awarded the Congressional Medal of Honor in WWI.

These recipients of our country's highest honor are accorded the honor of a salute by all military personnel. I realized how little I knew about military courtesy.

The Bloemfontein pulled away from the pier and the loud speaker announced the serving of mess for all hands. I waited until we cleared San Diego harbor before moving to an extremely long chow line that meandered around three or four decks. I knew I would starve before negotiating this endless line. At first the line moved almost imperceptibly; then faster than any chow line I had been in; the last hundred yards became a foot race. Amazingly I had accomplished the entire line in just over 10 minutes. The smell of food; the overheated galley area; and the pitching of the ship had taken a drastic toll on the would-be diners. I now joined the squeamish feeling group. Like hundreds before me, I too, suffered the Mal de Mer. Seasickness happens fast. I no longer wanted food. I wanted a ships rail or any place to relieve myself physically. Oh I was deathly ill. For the next six days I was as sick as I had ever been. On the seventh day I realized I was not sick and was in desperate need of food. Amazingly, I had lived. For my six days of illness, death had seemed the best way out. Now I was well. I had my sea legs and I actually wanted to eat. On all subsequent voyages, I never again became seasick. Obviously "sea legs" are permanent.

It was about this time we crossed the equator. The usual

festival with Neptune was an abbreviated ceremony but we were all invested as duly qualified "Shell Backs" and given cards to attest to this honor.

In our crossing of the Pacific Ocean, we experienced a storm of mammoth proportions. Our ship would climb one monstrous wave then slide down the back side of this mountain of water. Our ship was a large liner but these waves made it seem small. Because of the conditions below decks we spent a greater part of our time on the outside weather decks. When possible, we slept on these exposed decks also.

We were fascinated by the flying fish that seemed to abound in the southern Pacific waters.

We sighted no land or vessel during our entire voyage. We were assured the speed of our ship kept us safe from Japanese submarines. (We didn't believe this then, either.)

The Bloemfontein took us from San Diego to Auckland, NZ in 17 days.

NEW ZEALAND

After 17 days of high seas and storms the infamous Bloemfontein entered Auckland, New Zealand harbor and docked at the foot of Queen Street. We were fascinated seeing sharks as we came up the channel to Auckland. I had never seen a shark except in an aquarium. Auckland Harbor was a pleasant sight with the houses' red tiled roofs. The pier we tied up to was surrounded by a high metal-barred fence that restricted our desire to enter Auckland. We were able to disembark and move to this metal fence. New Zealand children would run across the street to buy us 10 cent meat pies. After the bad food we had been given aboard ship, the meat pies were unbelievably delicious.

The next day our regiment marched up Queen Street to the cheering of the locals. To these people, our presence meant more assurance the Japanese would not invade their homeland. We always felt welcomed in New Zealand. (This march up Queen Street was the closest I ever came to being in a parade.)

We boarded a train for a short trip to Whangarei, New Zealand on the North Island (New Zealand is made up of two major islands merely designated North and South Islands.) After detraining in Whangarei we were trucked a few miles to our camp at Mongadapari. We were housed in small huts, six men to a hut. This was a beautiful rural setting. Sheep herds ambled through our camp. Cows were fenced in next to our huts. The sheep were always accompanied by a sheep dog to keep them in a group.

The New Zealand sheep dogs were a remarkable breed. They acted like human shepherds showing great concern for the sheep in their flock.

One bright moonlit night about two o'clock in the morning, I was walking a guard post when a large herd of sheep passed through our camp attended by one of these wonderful dogs. As the lead sheep came even with me I slammed shut the bolt of my rifle and let out a loud growl. This spooked the lead sheep and he took off like a shot followed by a few hundred sheep. The dog leapt over the backs of the sheep until he reached the lead sheep. A quick twist of the lead sheep's head by the dog and the panic was over. I swear the dog looked at me and I understood the look to say, "Why did you do that?" Very clever, these New Zealand dogs.

VERNE KENNEDY

The same evening I confronted the panicking sheep I met the officer of the day, a young second Lieutenant named Verne Kennedy. He struck me as the loneliest guy in our camp. He asked me where my home was and when I said Chicago, he lit up with a smile. He countered, "I'm from Evanston, Illinois." We spent the next hour talking about the Chicago area. I had the distinct feeling he needed to talk to someone about home.

Over the next two years I saw Lt. Kennedy become Major Kennedy and when he died a few years ago, he was General Kennedy.

After the war Verne Kennedy and I shared the attic of the Sigma Chi Fraternity House and spent many pleasant evenings at the University of Michigan reminiscing about our war years.

IN THE HILLS OF NEW ZEALAND

We immediately began our training and practice firing. As we sat in forward observing positions we could watch our cannon shells pinpoint targets miles away. On one occasion Captain Gilliam centered an airburst over a lone pine and stripped it bare of branches. Utterly amazing accuracy.

We also began long distance hikes with full transport pack and rifle. We started at ten miles, then twenty miles, then forty miles. These were grueling tests of endurance. Our feet became covered with blisters; the fifty-five pound pack chaffed blisters on our shoulders that were further irritated by our rifle strap. If you dropped out of a hike you lost your liberty privileges. Few dropped out, but all griped.

After our stint on the Bloemfontein, I never seemed able to get enough to eat. I solved this by volunteering for mess duty. As a communicator, I was exempt from mess duty. This became the only mess duty I experienced. I tolerated it and Al Miller almost made it enjoyable.

Liberty in New Zealand was all we hoped it would be. There were dances, outings and socials. There were always enough women at these affairs. New Zealand had been at war for nearly three years and most of the New Zealand men were in North Africa fighting the German and Italians -- led by General Rommel. Both men and women of New Zealand were extremely friendly. A number of our boys married and brought their brides stateside (stateside was the usual reference word for America. Our ever-present dream was to "go stateside.")

I always enjoyed meeting the New Zealand women. Their cheery greeting of "Hello Yank." I'd always respond "Well said, Kiwi." This usually broke any ice that had existed.

The girls were so much like our girls back in the states there was no barrier to overcome. Oh, yes, their speech patterns were different, but beyond that, they were just friendly girls meeting friendly boys.

Churches and civic groups sponsored socials or dances. At these events, there did not appear to be any problem in meeting these friendly New Zealanders.

Training and hiking continued. The New Zealand Air Force would patrol our units and those not properly camouflaged were pelted with bags of bakers flour. These older aircraft flew real low and we could see the New Zealand pilots laughing as the flour bags exploded. We could almost hear them, "Jolly good fun, you know!"

CREATING OUR OWN FIREWORKS

Keeping in mind the fun we used to have with fireworks on the Fourth of July back home, we now possessed fireworks we never dreamed about. We had believed a cherry bomb or large five-inch firecracker was the ultimate noise maker. We now had two-pound blocks of TNT that paled all our former fireworks. On maneuvers, explosives were used to create a combat-like atmosphere. During these times we would take a few of the two-pound blocks of TNT and create our own Fourth of July. Kids will be kids.

While on the subject of our newfound fireworks, I am reminded of some other high jinks we enjoyed.

In every 105 millimeter Howitzer shell, there were seven bags of gunpowder. When the fire direction center called down the directions for firing the guns, one of the specifications was for the number of bags of powder to be used. The command from the Forward Observer would be "Battery adjust, shell H.E. (high explosive) Charge 5." This meant of the seven bags of powder in the shell, only the first five would be used.) Because our artillery was usually close to the front lines, the larger charges, six and seven, were seldom used. The large bags of explosives were usually thrown aside during the firing but were something to be destroyed before an accidental ignition happened.

The artillery men usually built a small fire and used it to dispose of its unwanted bags of gunpowder, one bag at a time. These bags burned in a flash of blue flame that flared high for mere seconds.

The fun occurred when someone stood back to the fire and one could flip a bag of gunpowder on the fire. The accompanying whoosh and flash of heat would move most to jump a foot. The perpetrator found great sport in this.

Another ploy was to drop a few rounds of 30 caliber ammunition into the fire. The accompanying bang would send most moving for cover. (The 30 caliber bullets would explode the brass casings, but not the propel the bullet. Just noise -- not much danger.)

Keep in mind, we were not idiots, just kids.

A LAND OF PLENTY

Things and food were very cheap in New Zealand. There were few things, but plenty of food. A meal of steak and eggs, chips (french fries,) salad, all the milk, tea or coffee was 38 cents including tip (two shilling or two bob.) A large crate of apples was $1. We didn't find the monetary system very difficult and even mastered the slang terms for New Zealand money.

Seafood and lamb were abundant. By any food standard, New Zealand was a land of plenty. Even in this land of plenty, the food in our Marine mess was bad.

We were told the deepsea fishing off the coast of Whangarei was considered among the best for Black Marlin. The inland waters were supposed to teem with trout. Unfortunately, we were never afforded the opportunity to test these waters.

USO-type shows provided by New Zealanders were one of our forms of entertainment. On one occasion, we were requested to join in with the orchestra and sing the Marine Corps Hymn. It became apparent we did not know the Marine Hymn past the first verse. This obviously embarrassed some higher ups, because the next day we received a directive that all hands would learn the entire Marine Hymn. I can't say if this was ever accomplished, because the issue never came up again.

LIBERTY HOUND

C.W Bowman of our "M" Battery had experienced a run of luck at the poker table. He had won 5,000 pounds. The rate of exchange placed the pound at 5 American dollars. Fortunately, Bowman sent most of this windfall back to the Bank of America. He retained enough to have a hole burned in his pocket by the abundance.

All this money and nothing to spend it on. We had the luxury of a hotel room in Whangarei. We had opportunity to share this largesse at restaurants, pubs, and service center dances. Strangely, pubs closed at 6 p.m., but we were not that interested in drinking, so it didn't matter.

We always made time for dances and meeting New Zealand's women. Life was good.

On one occasion, we went out of Whangarei to a dance in a neighboring town. After the dance, we got a ride to Whangarei, but the last bus had departed for Mongadapari. We had no alternative but to walk the seven miles back to our camp. Bowman and I were joined by Fred Johnson as we trekked back to camp. Fred fancied himself a great dancer and was very popular with the older New Zealand women. He claimed to be a professional dancer and certainly knew his way around the waltz, foxtrot, and tango. Unfortunately, Fred was wearing patent leather dancing shoes for our hike. After a few miles, he took them off and continued the walk in his stockings.

We made it back to camp just in time to answer reveille. It was then announced the order of the day called for a ten-mile hike. "Oh my," moaned Fred. Bowman and I faced a grueling day, but lived. As I kept claiming I couldn't make another mile, Bowman counseled "Don't walk a mile, just put one foot in front and then one more step. Just hang on."

I ended the tortuous day and kept my sanity by promising I'd soon be in bed for a long sleep. As I collapsed on my cot, Bowman bounced into my hut fully dressed for liberty. He said, "Get up and get dressed or you will miss the liberty bus." I groaned "Bowman, I am about to die. And all you can comfort me with is an offer

to go to town for a dance. Get out of here." The term
for Bowman was "liberty hound."

Small but easy-to-read signs indicated our time in New
Zealand was drawing to a close. Our mail was fresher
indicating we were on some kind of priority. We had a
pig roast with a couple of bottles of beer. We claimed
they were fattening us up for the kill. Actually this all
added up to our imminent departure.

We had a briefing by an Army intelligence officer. He
told us our 3rd Marine Division had been the main unit
available to meet any Japanese landing on Australia or
New Zealand. Now other reinforcements had entered
Australia lifting this guard duty and thus freed us for
action in the Pacific islands. This officer told us after
Guadalcanal, the 1st and 2nd Marine Division and the
Army's 37th Division were all decimated by Malaria up
to 85% casualties plus combat casualties. This was why
our 3rd Marine Division was so important at the crucial
time.

As usual our impending departure fired up the rumor
mill. We were off to Wake Island, Truk or Philippines.

Point to note: we were never, repeat never, told our destination as we boarded ship. This generated grist for the
rumor mill (or scuttlebutt as we called it.) The rumor
mill proved 100% wrong. Only after our ship was
underway were we told our destination and then only

hours before we disembarked. On combat landings we were briefed and given our specific assignments in plenty of time to make necessary preparations. (An exception had to be made for our Kaviang landing to be covered later.)

GUADALCANAL

Our ship from New Zealand to Guadalcanal was the USS Fuller, a combat transport. (A combat transport had davits to carry and unload landing craft and facilities for troops.) We always enjoyed life on Navy ships. The big plus was good food and dry quarters.

As we approached Guadalcanal, we were escorted by a flight of protective fighter aircraft. Our circling shepherds kept watch over us in these hostile waters.

As we moved slowly off Lunga Point, A Navy S.B.D. (dive bomber) flew past level with our ship's deck. The pilot and rear gunner waved and smiled -- welcome to "The Canal." They bounced past and I had the impression of a couple of kids out joy riding.

Our fighter plane escorts landed at Henderson Field. We had passed through "Iron Bottom Bay" unscathed. A battered ship's hulk lay beached off Lunga Point. We learned it was a Japanese cargo vessel that was run aground to keep it from sinking. The beached hulk remained unmoved and we viewed it when we departed Guadalcanal months later.

The island we were to call home for too long was a typical South Sea Island. A hot, damp, malaria infested, palm-tree-lined sinkhole. It had only one redeeming feature -- it was an unsinkable air base and staging area for future operations up the Solomon Island Chain. This made it an extremely valuable strategic piece of real estate.

As we arrived at Guadalcanal, the Captain of the Fuller came on the loudspeaker to announce "You and I will unload this ship."

As we slaved to get the Fuller unloaded, the mantra of the day was "The Captain isn't on our gang, he is on yours." These unloadings had to be accompanied at high speed because the night brought Japanese bombers. The ship wanted to be underway before dusk.

*U.S. First Division Marines storm ashore across Guadalcanal's beaches on
D-Day, 7 August 1942, from the attack transport USS Barnett (AP-11)
and the attack cargo ship USS Fomalhaut (AK-22). The invaders were
surprised at the lack of enemy opposition.*

OUR NEW HOME ON "THE CANAL"

After unloading the USS Fuller, we marched to our new
camp on Guadalcanal.

We pitched our tents in a coconut palm grove that we
learned was owned by Lever Brothers Soap Company.

The ground between the palm trees was overgrown with

weeds, varmints, rats and every kind of bug known to man. Our reinforced division of about 30,000 men made short work of policing (Marive term for cleaning) up the entire Palm Grove.

Our new camp was located next to Carney Field, a lesser known airfield on the "Canal." Just after dark, we experienced our first "Condition Red" or air raid. No big deal. One plane with a dozen bombs. We spent the raid in our fox holes. Subsequent rains filled our fox holes and future raids were spent next to the foxhole to permit immediate entrance if we determined the bombs were coming too close.

As I write about air raids, I may sound rather blasé, but let me assure you, at the time, we took the air raids extremely seriously. In my personal list of battlefield fears, aerial bombing and snipers headed the list. Aerial bombs, because of their enormous size, and snipers because of the swift unexpectedness of that single bullet.

When we landed on Guadalcanal in June of 1943 it was still a combat zone. Most of the land fighting was over but patrols still scoured the hills for stray Japanese. We had nightly bombings. I learned bombs do not whistle when they fall but make a whooshing sound. (Almost drowning out my prayers.) Malaria was our biggest problem and we were required to eat atabrine tablets to suppress its effects. This yellow pill gave us all a yellow pallor.

Because of the Japanese bombings, ships had to be unloaded fast and we were pressed into unloading ships. On one occasion we were sitting on the beach waiting our turn to go aboard the William Penn, a modest sized transport, anchored off of Guadalcanal. The ship was lit up because there was no condition red in effect (condition red was air raid.)

An aircraft with all its landing lights on was making what appeared to be an approach for landing at Carney Field. It took only one bomb or torpedo from this wily Japanese pilot's plane to sink the William Penn in a matter of minutes. We never heard how many men were killed. This was my first close-up sighting of a Japanese plane. We were all impressed by the audacity of this Japanese pilot.

The Japanese did not bomb us during the day on the "Canal." The night raids consisted of one or two bombers. We never saw mass flights of Japanese planes until we were on Bougainville. As bombers approached, a condition red was sounded by sirens and word of mouth. Then powerful searchlights scanned the sky until they found the plane and locked other searchlights on it. Once in these lights, the bombers did not appear able to evade them. Then the anti-aircraft fire began (usually very ineffective.) On one occasion, the Japanese bombers were held in the lights until a night fighter shot them down. We could see the tracer bullets hit the bomber and send it down in flames. As one bomber fell, the tail gunner fired his machine-guns wildly as in frustration.

The shooting down of a Japanese plane was occasion for cheering.

I have mentioned above, "Condition Red" meant air raid. "Condition Black" meant Japanese landing or incursion. We experienced "Condition Red" on numerous occasions but "Condition Black" only twice. More on this later.

For some unexplained reason, we had Marines who could call "Condition Red" before we got official word from the radar station. "Smiley" Burnett of our outfit was always ahead of the official sirens. Smiley was also able to tell when the bombers released their bombs. He said he could hear a click. Smiley never entered his foxhole until he heard the "click." I could never hear the click but Smiley's record was perfect. (So was mine; I was always in my foxhole ahead of Smiley.)

Troops from the Army's 164th infantry rest at a stand still at Guadalcanal.

FOOD

Since we have been overseas our mess hall food has been bad and unchanging. Breakfast was pancakes (crash pads) with syrup made of white sugar and a never-ending supply of unsweetened grapefruit juice. Next day powdered eggs, bread and coffee. Then back to pancakes again -- month after month. Lunch and dinner were also as repetitive as breakfast. No changes no exceptions. We always had bread, peanut butter, apple butter, and orange marmalade. I lived on this for month after month. There was always coffee.

Enough about food. Every serviceman felt their food could be improved. I recall an incident while in Miami Naval Air Station. I had just completed a breakfast of cereal, milk, two eggs, bacon and coffee. The two sailors across from me were griping about the way the eggs were prepared. I wanted to comment, but respected their right to gripe.

DEVIOUS WORK PATTERNS

There were the eager beaver type Marines throughout our Regiment. There were also many dope offs or masters at dodging work. The paragon of this latter group was C.W. Bowman who carried malingering to an art form.

Bowman openly professed his talent of avoiding work and freely dispensed his knowledge of work evasion (as he preferred to call doping off.)

Armed with a clipboard, pencil and ruler, he claimed he could walk through a standing parade with little fear of being challenged. He said he could accomplish the same shirking by merely carrying a hammer.

Unfortunately, Bowman's fame and techniques were broadcast widely and whenever he appeared with his basic clipboard and pencil, all the onlookers would break into laughter. Soon the Sergeants and others learned of the infamous Bowman ploy. It was painful to see genius frustrated.

A TIME FOR CHANGE

We were alerted we would be moving off Guadalcanal and into our first combat. Captain McCurry, now M Battery's Commanding Officer, spoke to us and told us we were ready to move out and if anyone wanted to transfer to another outfit make it known to the First Sergeant. I told C.W. Bowman and Lou Hum I was going to ask to be transferred. Both of these guys thought I was "asking for it" (trouble) and could end up in big trouble and still not get out of M Battery.

Rejecting the advice of this counsel, I told Top Sergeant

Warner I wanted to be transferred. In a few days I was told to pack up -- I had been transferred to H and S 12th Marines. This was the regimented headquarters Battery. C.W. Bowman thought I was the luckiest guy on Guadalcanal.

This actually turned out to be the smartest move I made while in the Marine Corps. I was now at a higher echelon and among some really great guys. A very happy move indeed. My enthusiasm is tempered only by the thoughts of leaving behind Lou Hum, Ron Norman, Vic Lukas, Al Miller, and C.W. Bowman. Fortunately the M Battery guys were just next door on the "Canal."

MY NEW OUTFIT -- HEADQUARTERS & SERVICE, 12TH MARINES (H AND S)

I met a new group of lifelong friends at H and S 12th Marines. Corporal John Wyly of Duluth Minnesota, Don Crickmore of San Diego, California, Harold Match of Tulsa, Oklahoma, Harold S. "Mayer" Kelly of Chicago Northside, Eugene "Ski" Gladowski of Chicago, Illinois, Jack Ladd of Hollywood, California. In this glamorous town, Jack cut the stars lawns. Captain Moss was our C.O. of the Communications 12th Marines. Sergeants Presser and Goffus gave us orders and kept us in line. Corporals Johnny Wardlow, William Coila and Red Edwards rounded out our chain of command.

Top Sergeant Thill ruled the enlisted ranks of H&S 12th Marines. Colonel John Wilson was commanding officer 12th Marines and Lt. Colonel Fairborn and Lt. Colonel John Letcher were his heavier staff, Captain Paul Moss, our Boss, Communications Officer.

The Radio Communicators were Jack Kerins, Dick Hannon, Christy, Pirtle, Jones, Milton Roberts. My first and lasting impression of my H & S 12th Marines was, I was proud to be among them. Other worthies were C.D. Brown, Bob Applebaum, and Verner Carlson.

The Communications code for the 12th Marines was "Decoy." The other regiments in the 3rd Marine Division also had "D" names. The 9th Marine was "Delta" etc. Our 3rd Marine Division code name was "Diamond." Charles Barrett, Commanding General 3rd Marine Division was "Diamond One." Colonel Wilson of H & S 12th Marines was "Decoy One." Lt. Colonel Fairburn was "Decoy 2," Lt. Colonel Letcher "Decoy 3," etc. Their code names permitted communications without giving a name.

PASSWORDS AND OTHER DISTRACTIONS -- SHIBBOLETH ALL OVER AGAIN

As I mentioned before, the passwords we devised contained the letter "L." It was known the Japanese could not pronounce the "el" sound.

Consequently, our passwords were: "Billiard Ball," "Pell Mell," "Ball Field," etc. The challenger would say "Halt Billiard" and the countersign by the one challenged would be "Ball."

This made for a pretty sound method to trip up the "el-less" Japanese. Unfortunately, even under the most dire conditions, those challenged had to purposely mess it up.

In practice, the challenger would say "Halt Pell." The humor driven American would respond, "So sorry, Marr."

One has to wonder if the ancient Gileadites had the same jokers.

Our housing on Guadalcanal was in eight-man pyramid tents. We were located in a coconut grove abutting Carney Airfield. The more well-known Henderson Field was next to Carney Field. Guadalcanal was right on the Equator, so it was always hot and it rained every afternoon. This assured us we were always sweating in a humid world. We had ample water for showers and our drinking water was supplied by "Lister" bags (large canvas and plastic) that held 55 gallons of water. We coped with all kinds of bugs, the most dangerous being the anopheles mosquito because it carried malaria. At first we wore mosquito head nets, but it became apparent we could not avoid mosquitos. Our cots were covered by mosquito netting suspended on four corner poles. Our ubiquitous rifle slung under our bed.

COMMANDER HORATIO WYLY

As I have said above, it rained every day. On occasion, we had rain all day and all night for days on end. These damp sessions were surpassed by monsoon-like downpours that flooded our camp. On one occasion as eve settled in our wind and rain swept tent, the water began to rise in our tents. Harold Match's cot situation in one corner of our tent was soon covered with water. Match laid half covered with water. He was doing a classic slow burn. As shoes from other tents floated past his cot Match used a bayonet to sink them. Jack Ladd seeing his cot would soon be immersed, moved his bed to the higher side of the tent. Corporal Wyly, our tent N.C.O, leapt up on the writing table that we had constructed around our tent center pole. Wielding a bayonet, one arm wrapped around the quaking center pole and shouting orders to his make believe sinking ship, "No one abandons this ship until I give the word. Avast you swabs, man the pumps. Hold fast men, I'm in control."

At this juncture in John Wyly's raving, the officer of the day and Sergeant of the Guard waded into our tent. A sight to behold, Wyly on the table wielding his bayonet, the lights in our tent flickering and now the new arrivals announcing "You may move into the dry ground of the officers mess." Awaiting an answer, I am certain they did not expect, the wild eyed Corporal Wyly's reply. "To hell with 'em. We choose to submerge." Even the immersed Harold Match roared approval.

SOME OF THE BOYS

As you might already suspect, we had some Marines that were different and stood out from the field green blandness of most of us. They lived in their own world or didn't quite fit into ours.

Of this cut was Lyle "Desperate" Deford. Brother Deford was by any standard an alcoholic. He had the topers inexplicable ability to find alcohol wherever fate tossed him.

I witnessed him making "Raisin Jack" aboard a naval vessel as we sailed to the South Pacific. He utilized a small wooden cask, originally meant to hold water on a life raft. A few handfuls of raisins, sugar, yeast, and water. A few days of fermentation and Lyle was under the influence. On Guadalcanal, he always had a cache of "Tuba," the local vintage of the palm trees.

Lyle's time with us was cut short (no pun meant) in a wood chopping incident. Lyle lost two fingers. It is reported he quieted the axe wielder by saying, "Thank you. That's the nicest thing anyone has done for me."

Lyle correctly viewed the accident as his ticket home and out of the service.

Then we have "Nigger" Bertrand.

Bertrand's sobriquet carried no ethnic implication, but stemmed from his way of greeting everyone. When one greeted Bertrand he always responded "Hey Nigger" or "Gotcha Nigger" or "At ease, Nigger." Bertrand, a New Orleans native, always had a smile and warm "Nigger" greeting for all.

On the serious or professional side, "Nigger" Bertrand was a card-playing artist. He could make a deck of cards dance.

He devoted most of his poker playing skill to the Army Casino on Guadalcanal. This casino was a quonset hut at Carney Field. This secret and exclusive gambling den provided a place for the elite dice and poker players to gather. All rank and commissions were left at the door. These were big-time gamblers. Only money and skill mattered here.

Nigger's skill prevailed. Major Kennedy told me he sent home a thousand dollars a month for most his time overseas. Pretty good on a private's salary.

PERSONAL HYGIENE

We were required to keep our camp and selves clean. We had to be clean shaven and only well-groomed mustaches were allowed.

CLEAN CLOTHES

Living in the tropics meant our clothes were constantly damp from perspiration or rain. This plus strenuous work and training routine called for frequent laundering of our clothes.

Our favorite method was boiling our clothes. This assured cleanliness and also provided an easy way to meet this need. We had hand-operated washing machines but they were always in a state of disrepair.

Aboard ship, we utilized the sailors method of draggin clothes in the ocean. Long strings held the clothes alongside the ship. The ship's movement and bouncing of the clothes in the ship's wake effectively clean the clothes. If left too long, this agitation could reduce your shirt to shreds.

We had frequent inspections and as a result our person and camp were kept smart. The Marines felt unkempt people or camp meant unkempt Marines. Cleanliness was a way of life in the corps. If one of our group failed to keep clean, it usually fell to those housed with him to correct his ways. As in the case of Rand vs. Kelly.

RAND VS. KELLY - A STUDY IN TACT

At times, cleanliness had to be pressed on individuals.

On one occasion, my good friend "Mayor" Kelly informed me as senior PFC in the tent I was dilatory in my duties. Having been hoisted to the lofty position of "senior PFC" I was immediately suspect of the Mayor's support. "Kelly, what has brought about this interest in my seniority?" I asked the smiling Irishman. "We have a problem that must be addressed. In a few words, Private Rand has not bathed in two weeks and in these tropics this is unacceptable." Kelly clarified my failure as "senior PFC." I reflected a few moments on this apparent problem before I suggested this was a problem that required a friendly approach instead of one dictated by the strength of one's rank. I reminded Kelly of his close-ness with Private Rand, having lived with him longer before I was transferred from M Battery. To my surprise, Kelly bought this reasoning.

We agreed we would both be in the tent when Rand returned that evening to assure Rand this wasn't just Kelly's assessment of his uncleanness. I counseled Kelly to be tactful and be ready to be supportive of Rand.

That evening Rand came in from baseball practice all

sweaty. He took his towel and wiped off the sweat. I could see Kelly was waiting for the right moment and probably weighing his words carefully. He then approached Rand and in bell-like tones firmly stated, "Rand, you stink. Take a bath." I moved in to support Kelly in what I hoped would be a short fight. Rand quietly grabbed his towel and headed for the shower. All I heard his say was "Okay." After Rand departed, all I could say to Kelly was "You are certainly a silver-tongued devil!"

Corporal Gaglia, the Colonel's driver, became an instant Private when he fired six to eight rounds from his Thompson submachine gun. Unfortunately, he was in his tent and in a non-combat area. Luckily no one was hurt. But the tent suffered an airing. The exhibition drew cheers from the entire battery. Private Gaglia cried foul!!

It was becoming apparent we were not long for Guadal-canal. Our mail was coming faster, we were given an allotment of two bottles of beer. Then the ultimate sign of pending combat -- a battery of medical shots. Always tetanus, but also other shots deemed necessary. Things were about to happen.

BOUGANVILLE

We were loaded aboard Navy transport vessels. The waters off of Guadalcanal were a hive of activity. Destroyers, a cruiser, transport ships were taking on supplies and troops. All this activity for the 3rd Marine Division. I was assigned to the APD Crosley (Attack Personnel Destroyer). This was a WWI destroyer outfitted to carry assault troops (perhaps 400.) It had three smoke stacks and was slimmer and smaller than present day destroyers. Being so narrow it cut through the waves and swells making for a smoother ride with almost no one seasick. Being narrow also permitted the Crosley to rock from side to side enough to let its screws (propellers) break water. Well, we were on our way, but we still did not know where.

The attitude of most of us on the Crosley was the same as when we were on maneuvers. I cannot recall any signs of anxiety. We were on a Navy ship eating Navy chow. This was our little share of heaven. It is hard to emphasize how good food can be when you have lived on peanut butter and apple butter for months. (Our mess hall food was the alternative.)

November 1, 1943 the landing at Empress Augustus Bay Bougainville Island was a near fiasco. Surf was running high enough to wreck landing craft. The Japanese bombed our transports (all missed.) We sat aboard the Crosley listening to the first assault waves report spotty resistance and that they were setting up a perimeter defense for the night. Our patrols had moved into the interior, but reported no in-depth defense. We remained on the USS Crosley until the next morning, November 2 1943, before joining our advance echelon on shore.

DIVIDING OUR FORCES

In the Bougainville Campaign as in other operations, the 12th Marines, as well as the other regiments of the 3rd Marine Division were not all placed on one ship. On our ship were members of the 21st Marines, 9th Marines, 3rd Marines. This was to assure if one of our transports was sunk there would be parts of the infantry, artillery, or engineers on another ship to continue the assault.

On the USS Crosley at Bougainville, these elements were company size. At Guam and Iwo Jima, we had battalion-size groups from the respective regiments on each transport.

Fortunately we never lost a transport ship during an assault landing.

Our perimeter was very narrow, extending just beyond the beach. Back of the beach, Bougainville became a jungle swamp.

Our first night was spent in the narrow strip perimeter that included two small islets Puruata and Torokina. My old M Battery was set up on Puruata Island.

In the evening of our first day, a New Zealand War correspondent talked to us to hear our stories of the first day on Bougainville and to learn about our homes and experiences in New Zealand. A very pleasant chap (I always spoke British after talking with them.)

Just after dark, the Japanese sent over bombers to work over our positions. They dropped quite a few bombs— but equally disturbing, they stayed over us for a long, ever threatening time. They seemed to concentrate on the two offshore islands. (I kept my fingers crossed for my M Battery friends.) Before leaving for the night, the bombers dropped a number of bombs all too near our foxholes. The next morning we learned one of those bombs had killed the friendly war correspondent. We heard his name was McPherson.

Word was passed that we were to move off the beach. We laid telephone wire through the swamp in back of the beach to our new bivouac area. Corporal Wyly, Kelly, Ladd and I actually laid most of this wire under the undergrowth up to our shoulders in waters, muck, and slime. After this lovely experience, we jumped in the ocean clothes and all. This swamp we had just negotiated seemed to be a great place for snakes. Fortunately we never saw a snake the entire time on Bougainville or anywhere in the Solomon Islands. Thank God!

Up to this point our casualties in the 3rd Marine Division were light but we knew the Japanese had 40 thousand plus troops on Bougainville. We also knew the Japanese were moving through the jungle toward our position. This was a time of preparation for the storm we knew was coming.

From the Frederick R. Findtner Collection (COLL/3890),
Marine Corps Archives & Special Collections

From the Frederick R. Findtner Collection (COLL/3890),
Marine Corps Archives & Special Collections

THE RUDE AWAKENING

There comes, to everyone in combat, a moment when they realize they could be killed at any moment. This may come as a quiet revelation or an all pervasive paralyzing shock. This neophyte in battle may freeze and be unable to comprehend or overcome this shock. With face drained of color, arms and legs shaking, and eyes fixed they make a sad sight. The expression "scared out of their wits" is most appropriate. This stunned condition passes and often with reassurance from those nearby him, they soon learn they too can cope.

The battle-tested veteran is scared but able to function as he copes with his fears. Be assured in death dealing situations, everyone is scared. Anyone not afraid is an idiot!

We all understand the first timers' fears, because we have all been there ourselves.

*From the Frederick R. Findtner Collection
(COLL/3890), Marine Corps Archives & Special
Collections*

*From the Frederick R. Findtner Collection (COLL/3890),
Marine Corps Archives & Special Collections*

OUR WORKING AREA

Our line laying took us to all parts of the perimeter. We hooked up lines to our firing batteries and helped maintain the telephone lines to our forward observers and infantry units, as well as to the shore defense 155 millimeter long toms. (Long larger cannons.) We enjoyed watching the Sea Bees build an airfield and a landing strip along the beach.

When our work took us to the ocean we never passed up the opportunity to swim and surf. We shied away from the jungle rivers and ponds because we had learned these harbored a fungus that settles in ones ears causing a painful and prolonged earache.

One of our swimming and surfing ventures turned into a life-threatening event. We had been using large rubber life rafts to ride the tremendous surf of the exposed beach. The Marine Raiders on their initial assault had used these rubber crafts on D-day. The surf was so great we could load three or four aboard these crafts and still be propelled through the surf at breakneck speed. We soon learned, as our rubber surfboard was about to be thrown over by the breaking wave, we exited astern never forward. The fun continued until we heard the "condition red" sirens. We decided to stay in the water reasoning the Japs would not bomb the ocean with all the targets exposed on land. Our attention was directed to a departing American convoy that was under attack by twenty or twenty-five Japanese planes. Our Navy gunners on the convoy and attending destroyers were taking a good share of the Japanese planes. We did not see any of our ships take a direct hit from the bombs. The Japanese planes, after dropping their bombs, circled around Empress Augustus Bay strafing targets of opportunity.

As the firing planes came closer and closer, we could hear responding fire from our Marines. In a roar the Japanese planes banked around Puruata Islet and headed down the exposed beach where we stood in the surf. At this point we ducked under water to assure we would not be hit by the strafing planes or friendly fire. As we emerged, the planes were directly overhead not more than 100 feet, and strafing this beach area. The roar of the planes and fire directed at them from the beach made for a loud confusing scene. As the Japanese planes moved down the beach, we became aware of another roar of an American Navy Corsair fighter plane that came over the beach area in pursuit of the Japanese planes. As he banked coming out of Empress Augustus Bay, he was at about 100 feet off shore when our Marine fire from the shore shot down this pursuing American plane.

The American plane landed in a Japanese held area of the beach. A patrol was immediately dispatched to rescue the downed pilot. He was retrieved and expressed regret about being shot down by his own Marines. Accidents like this were always a possibility in the heat and confusion of combat. We departed the beach glad we were able to walk away.

From the Frederick R. Findtner Collection (COLL/3890), Marine Corps Archives & Special Collections

OUR JUNGLE HOME

Our second bivouac area was carved out of the jungle. Strange creatures occupied the upper branches of the jungle. A small river ran past the front of our area and acted as a good barrier against a sneak attack. Like everyone else in our camp, Kelly and I spent one night crouched behind a machine gun in one of our camp's machine gun nest. The idea behind the two-man detail was one could sleep while the other stayed alert. Unfortunately both Kelly and I had super-sensitive imaginations and we were constantly at full alert by jungle noises we were sure were Japanese on the move.

As morning dew weighed down banana-like plants, the heavy leaves snapped and in our minds the whole Japanese Army was upon us. But alas, morning came and we shared a sigh of relief that we had held our fire and had not completely embarrassed ourselves. We laughed as we realized we had held the fort against particularly dangerous marching plants.

The ground in our camp was spongy. Some of our Marines attempted to sling jungle hammocks on good-size trees only to have them fall by the weight of the man. Keep in mind we were near the equator and it rained every day and our temperature always hovered over 100 degrees. Hot and humid.

From the Frederick R. Findtner Collection (COLL/3890),
Marine Corps Archives & Special Collections

In every combat area, there was never any movement after dark and no lights were permitted. It is hard to imagine how dark it can be under the jungle canopy. Once in our foxholes at night, anything or anyone that moved was fair game. The weapon of choice under these conditions was the hand grenade. The reason was that you didn't give your position away, a rifle or pistol shot would show a flash of flame when fired.

During one period of heavy rain, the roads turned into sinkholes four or five feet deep. Trucks bogged down and only caterpillar tractors could extricate them. We had many ways of coping with these wet conditions. We had our jungle hammocks. These hammocks were covered by a rubberized roof and mosquito-proof mesh on the side. In combat, we dug holes large enough to put our hammock and our body below the surface of the land. Consequently, during an air raid, we could remain in our hammock slung in a foxhole. We had ponchos of rubberized fabric that were waterproof. We also built up a tolerance for wet feet. Jungle warfare was perhaps the nastiest type—except the Russian winter.

One evening, I had moved into a supply tent to share a dry foxhole with another Marine. Just after dark, I heard movement next to our tent and could barely make our a hunched over figure coming out of the jungle. I took down an M1 rifle hanging conveniently on the tent center pole and quietly slid a round into the chamber. The figure moved closer and I had his head in my sights. He came over to the corner of our tent and threw the supporting tent pole holding the tent corner. This overt act saved his life. I felt the infiltrator was seeking a response to determine where we were. I opted not to fire a disclosing shot. After a short moment, the stealthy figure moved away—hopefully taking his patrol with him.

The next morning I saw activity in the jungle next to our camp. It was an army group that had moved in the night before. I went into the area and asked if anyone had approached the tent we had been in. A major told me he had. He was attempting to determine where his camp should be. I told him how close he had come to dying by moving after dark and that had he not thrown the corner tent pole down I would have shot him. The Major asked me if we didn't challenge before firing. I said sometimes but this close to the front he should not bet on it. We both smiled at this near tragedy.

Near tragedies such as this were repeated many, many times. When you have hundreds of armed men under combat tenseness and living in close proximity to friend and foe, accidents will happen.

From the Frederick R. Findtner Collection (COLL/3890), Marine Corps Archives & Special Collections

ANOTHER NEAR MISS

On another occasion, I was cleaning a .45 caliber automatic pistol when, I accidentally fired a round that struck two feet over a war correspondent's head. I was shocked, stunned, surprised all at once. "Smiley" Burnette quickly and calmly removed the pistol from my grip and threw it into a nearby foxhole. The rule in the force at that time was if you fired your piece and did not bring in a Jap, you lost a stripe. As the First Sergeant came storming back he was shouting, "OK where is the Private?" Smiley Burnette smiled his best and said "Sarge, you can sure tell when the Army comes ashore." The combat correspondent laughed the loudest and never said a word. I apologized for my dangerous act but the correspondent dismissed it as a natural occurrence in a combat area. Lest you think any misfiring was an isolated case, let me assure you it happened almost every day.

A great laugh was provided when one of our sergeants captured a Japanese. Unfortunately, the Japanese was an American doing work as an interpreter. The Sergeant had a hard time explaining the American uniform worn by his prisoner.

From the Frederick R. Findtner Collection (COLL/3890),
Marine Corps Archives & Special Collections

FLY BOYS & SEABEES

Our constant policing (testing & repairing) of the telephone lines took us to all parts of the perimeter. We
enjoyed watching the progress made by the Sea Bees on
the airstrip and roads. Within a few weeks planes were
landing and were being maintained at this airstrip
carved out of the jungle. The Seabees (Naval Construction Battalions) seemed older to us, but were fearless in
pursuit of their projects. Even under Japanese fire, they
moved on to their work.

On the airstrip were Corsair airplanes and P-40's with
their tails painted white. We were told the P-40's were a
New Zealand Air Force wing. The Corsairs were Pappy
Boyington's black sheep wing. The pilots always greeted

us mud Marines warmly and wanted to know what was happening on the front lines. When their work schedule permitted, we'd find them at the front talking to the infantry. Like our group, these pilots were just kids in a big job.

We had a "Condition Black" while on Bougainville, but it came to naught. Those kids in their Corsairs had decimated a Japanese invasion fleet of barges. They were fully appreciated by the "mud Marines."

We spent Thanksgiving and Christmas 1943 on Bougainville. As usual we had roast turkey with all the trimmings. An amazing culinary fête smack dab in the middle of a tropical jungle.

In appreciation for the job done by the Seabees on the roads and airstrips on Bougainville, the 3rd Marine Division erected a sign on the Piva Trail of Bougainville. It read:

> *So when we reach the Isle of Japan*
> *With our caps at a jaunty tilt*
> *We'll enter the city of Tokyo*
> *On the roads the Seabees built.*

We lost another Marine by an accident. He was burning trash and garbage using diesel fuel to keep the fire going. A mismarked 55-gallon drum of high octane airplane gasoline exploded when fumes hit the fire. Fortunately he lived but was badly burned. We never saw him after the accident.

C.W. BARKLEY - ATTORNEY AT LARGE

C.W. Barkley was a barracks room attorney. He became legally proficient in self-defense. He was a dope off that never got away with anything. If he tried a fast one, it would backfire every time. One of his more famous adventures began on Bougainville while C.W. sat on a forward observation post on the front lines.

A Marine Raider Patrol moved through the front line on a penetration into the jungle to assess the strength and placement of Japanese troops. C.W. grabbed his rifle and canteen and fell in with the patrol. He told his fellow Communicator on the F. O. (forward observation) he was going with the patrol and would be back when they returned to our lines.

In a few hours C.W. Barkley was at A.W.O.L. and AWOLIFOTE (absent without leave in face of the enemy.) There is no worse charge.

When Barkley returned, he was placed under arrest and told he would face Court Martial.

C.W. felt he had permission from the P.F.C. sitting with him on the F.O.. as C.W. reasoned he was a Private and he had told the P.F.C. (his superior) he was departing on the patrol.

C.W., the attorney, felt he had a good case. Lt. Colonel Kirk of the 4th Battalion 12th Marines differed with Barkley's opinion. C.W.'s next line of defense was the fact he had gone on a patrol toward the enemy and not away from the foe. In frustration, Lt. Colonel Kirk asked "Barkley, what am I to do with you?" Barkley suggested he be transferred. Lt. Colonel Kirk's ire was apparent when he challenged Barkley. "Transfer you? If I transfer you, I have to find someone who will trade me a man for a man. You are so well known, no one would swap me a man for you. However, in your case I'd take a warm bottle of beer or a broken baseball bat as a trade."

Barkley, protesting innocence, pulled a one-month sentence on the garbage scow off Guadalcanal. It was generally conceded colonels seldom lost to privates.

THE KNIFE THROWER

When there was a lull in our combat duties, we often played cards, usually poker. At one such game, I was seated near a palm tree. A new man in our organization began throwing his K Bar knife at this palm tree. I asked him to stop throwing his knife because it could bounce over in our direction. He proudly announced he never missed. I asked him if he wanted to bet on sticking his thrown knife 10 out of 10 times. He agreed and I tossed a ten-dollar bill out on the ground. He missed on the third throw. I asked him if he wanted another chance -- double or nothing. He agreed to try again. In the end of playing this aspiring knife thrower lost $140 to me in a very short time. I felt I should have told him throwing an unbalanced K Bare knife would task a professional knife thrower.

A few days after the knife throwing event, the knife thrower came to tell me he did not have the $140 to pay off his debt. He was being transferred out of our organization and asked would I take a non government issued Thompson submachine gun and call the debt paid. Submachine guns were a drug on the market in my present Marine role. But being realistic, it was the gun or nothing. The Thompson submachine gun was a beauty. It was a privately owned gun with a canvas carrying case for the gun, the round magazine and stick magazines. I was certain I could sell it to a Seabee or army man. I ended up trading it for a .45 caliber automatic pistol. In turn I sold the pistol to Private Bob Wolfe back on the "Canal" for $75. I have often wondered whatever happened to the Thompson submachine gun.

TOUGH MARINES, MUD & SHORT ROUNDS

When our infantry was experiencing extreme conditions on the front line of our perimeter, we were pressed into carrying ammunition to the "dug in" infantry. We found these guys sitting behind machine guns up to their waist in water. We did not envy them but we did admire them. As telephone men, we saw the entire scope of jobs under combat conditions. No one had it as tough as these infantrymen on the line. They always recognized us artillerymen because our telephone equipment carried our identifying code numbers. They always greeted us "Hey short rounds." The infantry knew the power of our guns but always feared we could err and drop a few "short rounds" on them. Knowing the deadly accuracy of our guns, I doubt if we misaimed. I can appreciate their concern because our barrages were awesome.

You may have noticed I never refer to our guns as cannons (which they really were.) We just never used that term. Our 1st and 2nd battalion were equipped with 75-millimeter pack Howitzers. A long-time gun in the Marine Corps arsenal. It was small and easily transported. Our bigger guns were 105 millimeter Howitzers. Our 3rd and 4th Battalions were equipped with these. Our regiment could focus nearly 50 guns on a given objective. Our artillery accounted for 50% of Japanese casualties.

This concentration of fire stopped Japanese attacks in their tracks and could decimate a suicidal Banzai attack instantly. Artillery preparation and pre assault bombardment paved the way for almost every infantry advance.

For these reasons the Infantry's reference to us as "short rounds" was a well-meant salute. We wore it proudly.

OTHER PROBLEMS

We experienced a couple of tremendous earthquakes on Bougainville plus aftershocks. The first quake hit early in the morning just after dawn. My jungle hammock slung in a foxhole, jerked and flipped me around like a bouncing ball. Half asleep I accused Kelly of jarring me awake. When fully awake, I realized no person could cause such a bouncing. The bouncing I had received and the shaking others had experienced seemed to be the only results of this early quake. Later in the morning as we stood in the breakfast chow line, there was another quake of mammoth proportions. We all had to get down on all fours or sit. It was impossible to stand. Trees criss-crossed violently and the ground came in waves. I am certain in a city this quake would have leveled everything. In our jungle world, the shaking of trees, rattling of pots and pans at the galley and shaking of the mess tent was all we could report.

The quake was bad enough but we were also aware we were at the foot of a smoking Mount Bagana volcano. We could imagine some potentially devastating problems. There were always those who sought immediate solutions to such problems. The thought was expressed that perhaps Palee, God of the Volcano, could be appeased if a few of our Marine privates were thrown into the caldera. It was generally agreed we could do with a few less privates. Need I say, we privates did not share this opinion.

MEDICAL CARE AND OTHER BENEFITS

Our regimental surgeon was a gynecologist. A strange specialty among a force of men. Actually, Dr. Anderson was a fine physician and had a group of aces supporting him. These medics held everyone's respect. In combat, the Medic had to stick his neck out while most laid low in their foxholes.

Our regimental dentist had to care for about 5,000 men. He worked with a pedal-driven drill under the most primitive conditions. He worked from early sunup until he had no light in the evening. Even under those dire conditions, his work was exemplary. After the war, several dentists commented favorably about his work.

From the Frederick R. Findtner Collection (COLL/3890),
Marine Corps Archives & Special Collections

CHRISTMAS

Well, it's Christmas; Christmas on Bougainville. (Hardly an inspiration for a Christmas Carol.) The married guys take it the hardest. Strangely, Bing Crosby singing "White Christmas" is more of a dirge than a morale booster.

We sit around consoling those in a blue funk and Christmas passed after the Marine Corps concept of the traditional "Turkey and all the fixins." The cook's try hard and we appreciate their effort.

Even the guys on the front lines are served well and fortunately there is a lull in the fighting.

Kelly and I have a telephone line out and we have to

press along the back of the 3rd Marines. They greet us with their usual smiles and protests of "short rounds."

We counter by expressing surprise that the infantry eats so sumptuously while the "short rounders" eat "C" rations.

Kelly and I walk away thanking our lucky stars we don't have the infantryman's lot in the the war.

All things considered, Christmas on Bougainville isn't that bad.

Life on the front lines stood in sharp contrast to the life in the rear areas.

On the beach area, a landing strip was bustling with landings and takeoffs; also hangers for plane repair were erected.

The front lines were in deep jungle and always wet ground. The Japanese made erratic pushes to test our lines and our resolve to hold them. Marine patrols venture deep into the enemy's lines in an effort to learn the Japanese Army's intentions. (We had to know where the 40,000 Japanese troops resided.)

Every effort was made to bring hot food up to the front line infantry, but only the coffee retained its heat in sealed urns.

Supplying the front was a never-ending effort and the final distances were hand carried.

We would often sit with the boys on the line and share a cigarette. We were always running into Marines we knew in boot camp or Communications School. I even ran into kids I had known in Chicago. These visits were seldom "afternoon tea" type meetings. The constant presence of snipers and sporadic mortar rounds kept one on edge.

The Japanese hit our lines and then faded back into the jungle. Our perimeter held and our 12th Marine Artillery responded as the infantry called.

Days became weeks and we were soon in our third month on Bougainville.

JUNGLE ROT

Most of us suffered a malady simply termed Jungle Rot. This manifested itself as an oozing sore that kept growing in size. It wasn't painful but one had to continually put sulfa powder on it before it became a major problem. My legs bear scars from this to this day. (This was indigenous to the subtropics and after leaving the South Pacific it ceased to be a problem.)

From the Frederick R. Findtner Collection (COLL/3890), Marine Corps Archives & Special Collections

RELIEF

The Army was landing in force on Bougainville and moving into the front-line positions. The Marine Infantry was moving back to the beach. It was our time to leave Bougainville. Scuttlebutt had it for certain we were heading to New Zealand for R. and R. Wrong again! We returned to Guadalcanal to our old camp in the coconut grove. Another cruel disappointment!

As we were climbing aboard our ship to depart Bougainville one of the Marines lost his grip and fell into the ocean. Weighted down by his pack helmet and rifle, he sank like a rock. A Navy Lieutenant standing on the flying bridge of our transport saw the man fall. Without hesitation he threw off his hat and dove among the milling landing craft right where the man had fallen. This was an extremely dangerous move to make his 40-foot dive between the landing craft and the transport. The diver surfaced having retrieved the gasping Marine. He was greeted with a chorus of cheers and applause for his heroic effort. We never heard, but all hoped the Lieutenant was cited for his heroic act that saved that Marine's life.

BACK ON GUADALCANAL

We found new replacements awaited us in our old camp. They were brought in to replace casualties and beef up our ranks for future operations.

OUR ATTITUDE TOWARD REPLACEMENTS

We were now veterans of our first combat. The replacements had not experienced the taste of combat. They would have to await their first experience under fire before they would be accepted as combat Marines. We knew there were many Marines in service of their country, but we distinguished between combat Marines and the others. We also knew there were combat soldiers and sailors and then there were the others.

To summarize our attitude toward our replacements it would be: we have been there and experienced the

brutal reality of war. You may join us—if you survive
the next landing.

SURPRISE

As I unpacked my sea bag I looked out of my tent at the
shower next to our tent. There to my utter amazement
stood a very familiar figure albeit naked. There stood
Jack O'Keefe stark naked and smiling. "Hey Swede, I've
been waiting for you." Jack O'Keefe, one of my dearest
friends from my time in high school. What a moment.
To find a dear friend on a remote South Pacific island, it
boggled my mind. "Where in the world did you come
from? How did you find me? Where are you located?"
The questions flowed.

Jack was now a Marine in the 21st Marines, 3rd Marine
Division, a neighboring outfit. Jack was newly arrived on
Guadalcanal as a Marine replacement. Upon reflection I
did remember Marion O'Keefe, Jack's sister, saying Jack
had joined the Marines. That he ended up on the next
street from me on the "Canal" seemed fate directed.

Jack O'Keefe's presence and humor were very uplifting.
The let down after combat experiences made our return
to Guadalcanal less than exhilarating. The arrival of
Jack into this miserable milieu was a timely antidote for
any depression or letdown I could have experienced.

Jack's sense of humor and ability to capsulize into his

own words that often reached beyond the apparent. A classic example of this was his reply to my query about his relationship with his fellow Marines in the 21st regiment. Jack replied tersely, "I don't know yet. I'm still sleeping on my socks." (lest they be stolen.)

The press of training did not permit Jack O'Keefe and me to spend much time together. The "mud sloggers" as we called the Infantry got the toughest shake in all military assignments. In combat they lived closest to the savage enemy; slept in water-filled foxholes; died in greater numbers; and when out of combat they are the first back in to the toughest training schedule. Why they call this branch "The Queen of Battle" escapes me.

Jack O'Keefe being new in the 21st Marines, was given the job of flamethrower. This was the least desirable of any infantry job. The equipment was heavy, clumsy, and very unreliable. More important was the inordinate attention given these men and their hell-sent machines, by the Japanese troops. Thus, they were on high priority for killing by the enemy.

I hardly have to tell you this assignment grieved Jack. I think this is the first time I heard the saying "It's a dirty job, but somebody has to do it." Jack's answer to all the attention his job evoked from the Japanese was "It gives me a warm feeling to be so wanted."

KAVIANG OPERATION

In the 12th Marines, we were training and involving our new personnel replacements. We had expected a lull after our return from Bougainville but it wasn't to be. We learned our next operation was already on the training schedule and it would require very special training.

We were told we would have to lay communication lines between some offshore islands. The islands were 400 yards offshore and our boats would be under fire from the shore. We would be working from rubber boats laying a heavy cable. This meant our artillery would be deployed on these islets to supply firepower for the assault on the main objective. It was hard to visualize how all of this would fit together. We had great concern about enemy fire from the beach as we paddled from islet to islet.

We spent a lot of time splicing wire cable together and expended a lot of rubberized tape to assure our splices were waterproof. We practiced letting out cable as we paddled rubber boats.

The work of wire splicing, training, and coordinating teams reached a feverish pitch. Each time we heard casualty estimates they were higher. We were told our objective was Kaviang in the Green Island group. This was the first and only time we were told the destination.

REPRIEVE

Then it all came to a sudden halt. It was over. The Kaviang operation had been scrubbed. All our training, splicing and conjecture were over. We breathed a sigh of relief. The talk of 80% casualties made this shut down a lifesaver. We later heard the operation had been the worst kept secret. Seems everyone had heard of the operation including the Japanese.

THE LONELIEST MARINE IN THE SOUTH PACIFIC

While on Guadalcanal, one of our worthies wrote to the Fort Worth newspaper and stated he never received mail and was the loneliest Marine in the South Pacific. To expand this plea even more, the United Press wire-picked this story up and the loneliest Marine's case was broadcast across the United States.

In a few weeks, the mail began to pour in. Dozen of sacks stuffed with pictures, letters, gifts, proposals of marriage, etc. This outpouring by American females was frowned on by the powers that be. The mailrooms were overwhelmed. The space devoted to this one person's mail was needed for more important war materials. Our boy pleaded it was beyond anything he envisioned when he wrote the letter to the hometown paper.

The Commanding Officer stated no more pleas would be made to American Mass Media.

From the Frederick R. Findtner Collection (COLL/3890), Marine Corps Archives & Special Collections

FIELD MUSIC

"And if the bugle gives an indistinct sound, who will be ready for battle?" 1 Cor. 14:8.

Our 12th Marines Regiment was plagued with poor buglers -- yeah, bad buglers!

Our men of field music could not blow reveille if their life depended on it. Their "Mail Call" often challenges "Taps" for its sadness.

Through the years our ears continued to be assaulted by the dissident tones. It was a problem never solved.

Fortunately, we gained reprieve in combat. It was decided to use the voice and not the bugle to wake people up. As you might imagine, no one really slept in combat which made waking the regiment rather easy.

It was widely believe the Marine Corps would have been embarrassed if the Japanese ever learned of this unsolved problem.

OUR BARBER

Out of combat, Dave Betheny was our regimental barber. His talent in the tonsorial art was limited but I guess the haircut we got was worth every cent of the twenty-five cents we paid. We found it did not pay to call to Dave's attention a nicked ear or missed trees. Dave had more pride than talent and no patience with detractors.

OUR PX

Then there was John Saylor the flint-eyed keeper of the PX. I might say the tight-fisted purveyor of Campbell's pork and beans. Our PX was devoid of any goodies. No candy or sweets. However we seemed to have a bottomless supply of Campbell's pork and beans. Unfortunately, we had few devotees of pork and beans so the supply never dwindled and the cans appeared eternal.

A MEERSCHAUM LINED PIPE AND ZIPPO LIGHTER

As I have observed our PX was usually bare of any interesting items. However, on one occasion there was a Meerschaum lined Kaywoodie Pipe I coveted. Unfortunately, the man ahead of me in line was Private Davidson, who purchased this brier beauty. Rats!

Over the next few months I envied every puff Davidson took on the nearly-mine pipe. I took heart feeling perhaps he was breaking it in for me.

The word passed Davidson was being shipped to the states. After I pointed out Meerschaum lined Kaywoodie Pipes were available all over the United States, Davidson agreed to sell me the long sought after pipe.

I now find it hard to believe I would be interested in a used pipe. It tells me how completely we were deprived of luxuries while in the Pacific.

Another sought after item was a cigarette lighter. I offered Private Scott fifty dollars for his beat up Zippo lighter, an offer he turned down with disdain. I felt it was a reasonable offer, after all it was one months salary.

OUR CHAPEL

We always constructed a chapel in our camps. This was used for all religious services with no restriction on any

STILL A PFC: A COMBAT MARINE IN WORLD WAR II

form of worship. We had Catholic, Protestant and Jewish services in this same chapel. Very ecumenical.

GETTING RIGHT WITH GOD

I shared this spirit of ecumenism and on occasion attended Catholic, Jewish and Protestant services. This was no time to have doubts about who had the right road. In one service I attended with Al Miller, this red-haired Rabbi talked out of the side of his mouth in a distinct Brooklyn accent. He admonished us to "get right with God." For months after this I would challenge Al to "get right" doing my best side of the mouth Brooklynese.

BELATED GREETINGS FROM YOUR UNCLE SAM

Our entire Marine Corps was a voluntary organization until late in the war.

This volunteer status provided our leadership with the catchphrase often cited if we griped about food, housing, etc. They merely reminded us "you asked for it!"

Everyone enjoyed posting their draft notices forwarded by their parents or family. We often wondered how the Draft Boards learned we had skipped the country aided and abetted by the US Marine Corps.

REPLACING CLOTHING OR SURVEYING RAGS FOR NEW

I have mentioned the flint-eyed dictator of the Post Exchange, but his hard-heartedness was not in the same class as that of Sergeant Jewsbury of the Quartermaster tsardom.

The process to obtain new clothes was simply stated. You traded worn out garments for new garments. With this statement all simplicity ended.

To approach Sergeant Jewsbury with the naive notion you could obtain new clothes would be like going to our mess tent and expecting a gourmet dinner with fine wine.

Always ready to defend his domain, Sergeant Jewsbury could always be expected to greet you warmly. "Now, what the hell do you want?"

"Hi Sergeant. I have a couple of pairs of socks and some skivvies I want to survey for new replacements."

"Peterson, do you think the Marine Corps exists to supply you with new clothes!?!" Sergeant Jewsbury was in a good mood or perhaps better than usual.

In his role as the Marine Corps last stand against our excesses and opulence, Sergeant Jewsbury inspected the four socks I proffered. "This hole isn't that bad."

I suggested the hole in the sock was big enough to pass a watermelon through.

My observation was ignored as Jewsbury attempted to match at least two out of the four holey socks to make one pair that could stand more use.

Apparently Sergeant Jewsbury was stumped as he places his fist through each hole. He turned his attention to the frayed skivvies (undershorts.) He did not seem to be impressed with the buttonless shorts with large holes in the seat.

With a deep sigh of regret he issued me two pairs of socks and one pair of skivvies. He deemed one pair of skivvies still serviceable. Jewsbury sought some victory out of each encounter.

To give you an idea how tight the Raj of the Quartermaster was, our original issue of clothes in boot camp was white tee shirts, white skivvies, and white socks. In 1942, the Marine Corps in its wisdom determined green underclothes and socks would be more difficult for the enemy to see during combat. The order was cut that as the underclothing and socks were worn out they would be replaced with the new green issue. At my discharge in 1945 all my underwear and socks were well-worn white. I strongly suspect that some Marines at this late date are still wearing white underwear and white socks. In some quartermasters warehouses there are green shorts, tee shirts and sock piled to the ceiling dating back to 1942 when it was determined green was the preferred color. Change comes slow in the Corps.

TELEPHONE COURTESY

In the Marines there was a very strict rule that you did not use profanity on the radio or telephone. There were even stricter rules governing relations between low echelon staff and higher echelon staff.

All this strictness came to a head while I was manning a switchboard on Guadalcanal.

A little after 2200 hours (10:15 pm) I received a call from an officer in the 4th Battalion demanding I place him through to the Regimental Officer of the day.

The phone in the Officer of the Day's tent was answered, "This is lieutenant _____" Before this reply could be finished the overly irate officer from the 4th Battalion cut him off saying "Lieutenant, my ass. This is Captain Sharpe at 4th Battalion H & S. Get your ass in gear and act like an Officer of the Day. I'm trying to sleep and I hear noise from your camp." This explosion was greeted with an ominous moment of silence. Then in a calm, measured overly quiet voice came the response. "This is Lieutenant Colonel Fairborne. I am in the G-2 tent and H & S 12th Marines. I expect you here in 4 minutes." Click. The phone went dead and I suspect the Captain wished he was.

In my strategically placed switchboard tent, I saw the 4th Battalion Captain enter the quarters of Lt. Colonel Fairborne. I heard the Colonel ask the Captain if he was aware of the proper protocol in using Communications gear in the Marine Corps. The tent flap closed at this point, but the Captain did not depart for almost an hour.

A smiling Lieutenant Colonel Fairborne came to our switchboard tent and requested a copy of "Rules & Regulations Governing Conduct on Marine Corps Radio & Telephones" be sent to Captain Sharp of the 4th Battalion." Over and out.

THE LIFE OF A COMBAT LINESMAN

We were told in Communications School our role in combat would be very precarious. The nature of our role, in keeping our telephone lines open, required us to move about while other luxuriated in foxholes or other sedentary positions.

In combat, this proved correct. Strangely, our safest area of operation was near the front lines. Our Infantry kept the enemy at bay but in rear areas we were subject to mortar and artillery fire.

The great truths one quickly learned was there was no "safe" place in our combat area. Although aware of this, you had to do your job and work with others that carried the same burden. It was after combat in rear area you came to the full realization of a freedom from fear. The outward manifestation was a heightened feeling of elation; laughing too long at not too funny situations, relating dangerous combat situations that now were told as laughable.

To the new Marine replacements, we were considered "Asiatic," a term applied to those deemed overseas too long or a little short on good sense. Actually, we were celebrating being alive and having beat the odds. (This concept of beating the odds wore thin as we went from one combat landing to the next.)

ANOTHER MOVE

Things seemed to be heating up. The shots were given, we received the telltale two cans of beer ration, and our mail was very recent. We awaited our orders to move out.

Before we move on, let me comment on the beer allotment that meant we were on high priority. In our entire time overseas I imagine we received between 15 or 20 cans or bottles of beer. Spread this over two years and you can see we were not awash in alcoholic beverages. The only other acquisitions of alcoholic beverages I can recall was 190 proof alcohol from the torpedo storage center on the "Canal." This cost $20 a quart. The original intent was for this alcohol to propel torpedoes. The reason for this alcohol was a party celebrating our departure from Guadalcanal. Certainly this was deserving of a grand party.

TUBA, ANYONE?

While on the subject of alcohol beverages, I must comment on the acquisition of a potent drink extracted from the coconut palm by some of the more determined toppers. One climbed to the top of a coconut palm and inserted a small bamboo pipette into the base of the palm heart; let this sweetened juice drain slowly into a large bamboo cup cylinder (about 2 feet long.) This was left positioned in the palm tree to ferment for a few weeks. The resulting drink was potent and called "tuba" by the natives. Interestingly when the large cup containing the "tuba" was retrieved from the palm tree, it had a top coat of three or four inches of dead bugs in the bamboo cup. The hearty sots spooned these bugs off before drinking the "grand tuba."

THE DISTANT DRUMS

Guadalcanal was rapidly sinking into a backwater position in the Pacific War. We had taken Bouganville, the

1st Marine Division had taken Cape Gloucester on New Britain Island, and the 2nd Marine Division had taken Tarawa. We anticipated another move to the Central Pacific. VIP's were also on the move.

ELEANOR!

I noted a transport plane as it landed at Henderson field escorted by six fighters. This indicated we had a new VIP on the "Canal." That evening as we were driving back to our camp we were pulled over by MP's and told to stay aside until told we could move on. It was dark when an open staff-car passed. I could not see the passenger but heard the distinct voice of Eleanor Roosevelt. I reported this to our camp and in a few days Mrs. Roosevelt's trip to Guadalcanal was in the world press.

USS CRESCENT CITY

At embarking time the orders always came fast. "Pack up, fall in, move out." Orders didn't take long to be executed. We were back aboard ship again destination unknown. Our ship was the USS Crescent City - a combat transport. We were boarded as an advance group. Fortunately we were aboard this ship almost a month before the main body of troops came aboard. This was by far the best ship we had been on during our entire time in the Pacific. Good food, great quarters, and a ship's crew that treated us as guests rather than intruders. We all pulled mess duty—but who cared. We were on a floating bit of heaven with sunny-side-up eggs, ice cream, and a ham dinner I still talk about. What a way to run a war! Actually this marked the end of our small South Pacific War.

. . .

The Rear Echelon

Whenever we departed on another combat mission, we left behind a group termed "rear echelon." This group had the responsibility of taking down our tent cities, handling and loading our seabags, and all other materials and equipment the assault group left behind. The "rear echelon" would then follow us and land after our objective had been taken. In the case of Bougainville and Iwo Jima, when we returned to Guadalcanal and Guam respectively the "rear echelon" had merely a maintenance job until we returned. I always thought it strange the "rear echelon" received all the shots the assault team were given. Tetanus, Typhus, Cholera, etc. The Corps was generous in creating sore arms.

A Nice Little War

As we were about to depart Guadalcanal, I reflected on the war we had seen while in that area. Our Navy suffered devastating losses early in the South Pacific war. The landing on Guadalcanal was the cause of more Naval action and again our Navy took its share of losses. Then the area moved into a relative calm.

The Japanese were over-extended. They had long, dangerous supply lines.

The United States had suffered great losses in the early months of the war and was striving to meet its obligation in a two front war with the stated objective of Europe first. In the South Pacific we had limited forces. A Navy licking its wounds. Three Marine Corps Divisions. Two or Three Army Divisions and a patch work Air Force whose fighters were inferior to the Japanese Zero. Not a very pretty position to be in.

One of our saving factors was Japan's need and desire to consolidate its early territorial gains. The tremendous losses by Japan at the battle of Midway was also an arresting force.

Of our three Marine divisions, the 1st and 2nd Marine Divisions came off Guadalcanal with 75% to 80% casualties mostly from malaria. The Army divisions had come off of Guadalcanal with similar casualties mostly from malaria. Divisions numbered about 16,000 men.

When one looked at their meager force facing a dominant Japanese Navy and an army of two million, the picture darkens even more.

While the fiasco at Midway and loss of Guadalcanal were stunning blows to expansionist Japan, they provided a breathing spell for the extended American forces. It was during this period we served in the South Pacific. Early 1943 to early 1944.

During this period we knew each Army, Navy, Marine, and Air Force unit in our area. We shared a camaraderie of being out on the line and never too sure we could hold it.

We were in awe of the North African and European war where Armies of millions clashed. We knew of the armadas of ships and massive air raids by both sides. When we talked of divisions, Europe talked of armies.

However in our "me to" position in the South Pacific where we had to do with what was left over from the European demands, we turned our war from a defensive position to an offensive position.

Small World

In our small war, we had some unexpected perks. We knew our neighbors. We greeted out "dog face" friends (Army) and "Swabbies" (Navy.) No longer rivals, but friends, sharing mutual miseries. (Pre-combat hostilities long-forgotten.)

A friend, Corporal Thurman and I, attempted to visit a friend of his from the Dakotas, Joe Voss, the fighter ace. We learned Vos was no longer at Henderson Field. The point I wish to make is that we could locate and visit friends. Guadalcanal wasn't that big.

I was surprised when Les Knox, a Chicago friend arrived for a visit. He sported the stripes of an Army Staff Sergeant. At one time, Jack O'Keefe and I shared the "Canal" with six Chicago friends. Custer Redmond, a friend from Hyde Park High School also joined us.

It seemed at the time Guadalcanal was populated by Chicagoans.

There were other extraordinary opportunities available for your free time or a pleasant Sunday afternoon pastime on the "Canal."

If you were checked out (qualified) on fifty caliber machine guns you could go on air raids up the Solomon chain hitchhiking on raiding aircraft. I never took advantage of this hazardous pastime feeling I had enough of the war on my plate as it was. Those who did take the ride reported the extremely heavy flak they experienced over Rabaul. I cannot recall anyone asking for a second trip.

Where Has All the Interservice Rivalry Gone?

At this time each branch of the service appreciated the other's piece of the action. We walked tall among our brethren in arms. There was always time to greet one another. "Hey Marine, you going anywhere?" "Naw we are here to look after you Army boys and keep the Jap's from scaring you off this rock." "Keep it up Marine, but us Army boys are carrying you along for laughs." "Hey sailor, was your old man in World War I?" "Hell, no he was in the Coast Guard."

These jibes if made in the pre combat era would have led to a fight. Out here in our Pacific the smiles behind them overwhelmed any hostility. We heard a lot of good spirited kidding, but basically we were all aware of being together in our nice little war.

Time on Our Hands

Our biggest source of entertainment was card games. The gambling went on even though most of us never had money until payday. In this era of no money, credit poker (jawbone) games flourished. Our local entrepreneurs were John Wyly and Harold Match. They ran the jawbone game, supplying cards, table, chips, and kept the books for a small cut of each pot. They also played. Wyly played close fisted, Match wanted to play each hand. I can't recall their becoming wealthy but they provided a way for us to play on credit.

Not all our games were on credit. At payday the games were big time. If one won at the company level, he could move up to the bigger games at the Division Headquarters. The winners at this level could progress over to a Quonset hut at Carney field where the big time winners settled both poker and dice championships.

Yes, Guadalcanal was getting more sophisticated. We even had a Red Cross canteen off the main drag of the "Canal." They only had coffee when I went there. It was a dime a cup. Many of our boys thought it should be free. The Red Cross had its critics. I never asked the Red Cross for anything, so I have no first-hand opinion.

And to think we are now leaving all this behind us on the "Canal!"

BACK ON THE USS CRESCENT CITY

Life on the Crescent City was an extended R&R (rest and recuperation.) We were treated as part of the ship's company as we awaited the embarkation of the main body of troops, we cruised around Guadalcanal, Tulagi, and Florida Islands. We had the feeling something was holding up the operation. We had few complaints for our extended time aboard this fine vessel. We had general agreement that as long as this soft life and good food continued they could keep the war on hold, indefinitely.

With the ship's crew, we were taken to Tulagi Island for a beer party and games (baseball, horseshoes, etc.) The beer and good food made this a day to remember. During these lush days I often thought I should have joined the Navy.

As I have said we were treated as part of the ship's company and this meant we were subject to the Captain's inspections. As the Captain approached our assigned station, he commented to the staff accompanying that there seemed to be enough Marines, but too few Naval personnel. He asked me why the Naval personnel was absent. I told him they were below unable to stand inspection because they were seasick. The

Captain laughed and said, "Thanks Marine. There is something wrong with this picture."

I responded with a smile and a short "Aye, Aye."

All good things must come to an end. The word was passed that the rest of the Marines were coming aboard. Part of the 21st Marines, 9th Marines, 3rd Marines, and 12th Marines came aboard. Other parts of these units were on five or six other transports as we departed Guadalcanal in convoy. At the time we did not realize we would never see the "Canal" or the South Pacific again.

As we leave the "Canal" a short comment about the natives of these islands and the glamorized south sea women. In a world, "UGLY!"

Related Tragedies

One of our cooks received a request from his wife to approve her entrance into a government hospital to deliver her baby. The cook was devastated because at the time, he had been overseas for sixteen months.

Unfortunately, his grief was short lived. He was killed on our first night on Guam.

To The Central Pacific

We were now sailing in a convoy of six transports and three destroyers. We also had the comforts of an air patrol part of the way. It was June 1944 and we were heading to the central Pacific, but an undisclosed location.

We were briefed by a Naval Officer as our small convoy moved ever north. (We could not see the Southern Cross in the starlit skies.) This officer told us we would awake the next day in Eniwetok Atoll. This tremendous lagoon was formed by coral atolls and provided a safe harbor in the mid-Pacific Ocean. He told us when we came on deck in the morning we would see one of the greatest armadas ever assembled.

Eniwetok Atoll

The next morning the sight in the Atoll was breathtaking. As far as the eye could see were aircraft carriers, battleships, cruisers, destroyers, troop transports and every imaginable type of vessel. The scene was overpowering. Eight short months ago we had landed on Bougainville with a cruiser and six destroyers to shell the beach. Now we were preparing for an invasion with this vast Armada to lead the way. Let me call to your attention, this was June 1944 and on the European Continent "D Day" was occurring employing the "greatest armada" ever. Unbelievably, here we sat in Eniwetok Atoll surrounded by a massive assemblage of ships "as far as the eye could see."

Also remember -- at this point we did not know where we were going to land. After we moved out of the Atoll in a grand convoy we were told our destination. We were heading for an island called Saipan in the Marianas.

Saipan Island - Floating Reserve

The 2nd Marine Division and the 4th Marine Division were the assault group. Our 3rd Marine Division was designated "floating reserves" for the invasion. This meant we were on standby and would not land unless we were needed. We stood off Saipan for a number of days before we pulled away and returned to Eniwetok Atoll. We continued to follow the fighting on Saipan by radio and written dispatches. We knew how rough the Marines were having it on Saipan. We obviously did not miss Saipan by much.

GUAM

We spent only a short time at Eniwetok Atoll. We were given the opportunity for swimming and exercise on the island of Eniwetok.

Once again we were underway. (It had to be Wake Island this time.) Alas, the rumors proved wrong and we were told we would be assault troops for the retaking of Guam. This would be the first, occupied American territory retaken from the Japanese. We were going to make our landing on Asan Beach between Asan Point and Adelup Point. A Marine Brigade (two regiments) and the Army's 77th Division would land at another point on the Island of Guam. We were told Guam was heavily defended and that our assault would be warmly met. (Very discomforting.) This came as no surprise and we reflected "they don't get any easier."

AN AWARENESS

As I have related, we wore our religion on our sleeves. We did not hesitate to acknowledge our religious needs. The Catholics wore medals and carried rosaries; Protestants carried small Bibles, some with a sheet of steel attached. (I considered this slight hedge almost sacrilegious); Jews never seemed to have any physical devices, but we were aware of their piety.

Just prior to our disembarking for an assault on a defended beach, the men flocked to last minute religious services. No one kidded about their need to be on the right side of God.

The unknown future loomed dark!

THE ASSAULT ON GUAM

The morning of D-Day we were awakened at 3:30am. We were immediately fed and then assembled at debarkation stations. Our debarkation station was up forward on the starboard (right) side of the Crescent City. The ship was abuzz with moving gear, lowering landing craft, and jockeying cargo for off loading. We fidgeted around at our designated places; checking packs, loading our weapons, tightening straps and making sure when the word came we were ready to go over the side. We were told the password for the first day and night was "Billiard Ball." Our passwords always contained "L." We were told the Japanese could not pronounce "el."

The breakfast we had been served was a disappointment. We had eaten so well on the Crescent City we expected steak and eggs as our final meal aboard. Perhaps, you can appreciate our surprise and upset when we were served white navy beans (unseasoned) bread and coffee. There was open grumbling in the ranks. Obviously this discontent reached the Captain of the Crescent City. The loud speaker broke forth. "This is the Captain. I hear you Marines were disappointed in the breakfast of beans we served you. This was not my choice. I have steak and eggs aboard and we were prepared to serve this for your last meal aboard. However, I was informed, by those who know about such matters, that the beans would stay with you longer as you face this long day. I wish you all God's speed in your mission and I salute the gallant Marines we are putting ashore today."

Our wait at our debarkation dragged on. There was a call for Crew's breakfast. (Those not involved in tending landing craft.) Because of my length of time aboard the Crescent City, I knew my way around the ship's passages and knew most of the cooks in the galley. I bolted for the galley and ran to the front of the long chow line. They were serving meatloaf. I grabbed a couple of slices of bread and asked the sailor passing out the meatloaf for a slice. He said "Beat it Marine. We already fed you." The Navy Chief Cook stepped forward and pushed the surly sailor aside. With one sweep of his hand he grabbed a towel and wrapped up a half of a meatloaf. Handing it to me he said, "Thanks Marine. Stay alive." I responded to him as I ran for the door. "Thanks Chief, I owe you." The chief acknowledged some kind remarks from the onlookers.

I ran back to my boat station and just had time to pack the meatloaf into my backpack.

On Asan Beach the Naval fire seemed to intensify. The Battleship Pennsylvania was covering our landing beach with broadsides and also a lighter cannon that hit my ears like the crack of a whip. The destroyers and cruisers were also continuing their shelling points along the beach. The battleship USS Pennsylvania (CBB-38) was an old friend. We could always recognize her by her clipper-shaped bow.

OVER THE SIDE

Now it happened fast. Move out! Down the landing nets into rocking Higgin (L.C.I.) boats. (Landing Craft Infantry.) Once loaded we moved away from the Crescent City and began circling preparatory to making our assault-wave run to the beach.

First flag on Guam on boat hook mast. Two U.S. officers plant the American flag on Guam eight minutes after U.S. Marines and Army assault troops landed on the Central Pacific island on July 20, 1944.

INITIAL ASSAULT WAVES

The initial assault waves move away from the transport ships and form circles. As other assault crafts are loaded, they join the circle until sufficient forces are ready for the dash to the beach. When the required assault troops have filled the circle, a signal is given and now the circles break into a "line of departure" and move to the beach.

As we stand in the landing craft, crouched below the boats' sides, we are all hoping to live through the next hour. We are scared, excited, proud, scared, anxious, unsmiling, scared, ready for the worst, scared, our greatest fear is that we'll show our fear. Oh, have I mentioned we are big-time scared?

The attending Naval shelling continued at a quickened pace. Airplanes dove to drop bombs and strafe the beach area.

Then the bombardment moved to the back of the landing area and on to the surrounding hills. We expected to ride the LCI craft to the beach, but just off the beach we were told our LCI would not cross a coral ridge. We were loaded into awaiting amphibious tractors and now we moved toward the beach at a slow pace. The Japanese had anticipated our coming ashore and began firing artillery and mortars. We felt like sitting ducks because the amphibious tractor seemed to inch along. After an eternity we hit the beach. The tractor driver yelled for us to "get off and do it fast." He was anxious to get back beyond the Japanese fire.

I climbed over the side of the tractor and prepared to jump into the water. We appeared to have stopped about 20 yards off the beach. As I prepared to jump, a mortar shell hit on the other side of the tractor. I leaped into water I thought to be five-feet deep. It turned out to be very shallow - about two-feet deep. Loaded down with pack, rifle and communications gear, I hit real hard. I felt like my back was broken. I ran for the beach in a half crouch. Mortars and small arms fire were zinging past us. Men were down on the beach, hurt and dying. The cry for medic was heard from a dozen directions. I dropped behind a sandy rise on the beach. Next to me were Skutel and Seppi.

This was their first combat and they were getting a tough indoctrination. A Lieutenant from our Battery dove in next to me. He recognized me and said we were to get off the beach. "Head inland to your assigned area." He added, "Peterson, keep your head down!" and a smile.

To move across the flat, open area ahead of us under the present small arms and mortar barrage seemed madness. I asked Skutel and Seppi to follow me and we headed for the mouth of a river to our left. We paralleled the beach until we came to the small stream and then headed inland behind some low trees and any other cover we could find. Between us we had a field switchboard, several rolls of combat telephone wire and field telephones. We continued along the stream, but not down in the stream bed. We eventually came to our designated 1st base camp on Guam. We were among the first there.

A US Marine is given water as he lies on a stretcher with bandages covering his wounds after seeing action during the 1944 Battle of Guam.

Marines show their appreciation to the Coast Guard during the invasion of Guam during World War II

Forward, Ever Forward!

From this vantage point I could look back at the beach over a low area that was a dry rice paddy. The main infantry body was crossing the rice paddy under heavy mortar and small arms fire. I could see a man fall—but immediately, another took his place. The infantry wave moved relentlessly and irrepressibly forward. I could see medics running to the fallen.

If I wasn't so afraid I'd probably stood up and cheered. A very moving moment. "The Marines have landed!" I could see the infantry scouts already in place at the base of the hills surrounding the rice paddy urging their fellow Marines to take up forward positions. I stood awed by the scene and the heroes I was observing.

As I write this, forty years after the event, I still feel proud that I could have been with these brave men that were crossing this deadly beach and flat rice paddy.

"Peterson." I awoke from the surrounding scene of bravery to see Corporal Wyly gesturing. Wyly was pointing toward the beach and screaming for me to get the second battalion telephone line off the switchboard and out to their location. I told him I'd have to go alone because Kelly had not shown up as yet (We had this responsibility.) He countered I should take off and when

Kelly showed up he'd send him after me. A bad thought crossed my mind. "IF Kelly shows up." I needed to carry two reels of combat wire (light weight) and hoped it would get me to the 2nd battalion. I knew where they were supposed to be, but the way the beach was being covered by Japanese mortar fire, anything could happen. I took off with the river bed to my right. I hadn't gone far when I ran into Kelly and Harold Match lying behind some logs. "Hey Kelly -- what are you doing taking a rest?" Kelly replied, "Match has been hit." I looked at Match but he didn't look too bad off until I saw his bloody back. A sharp piece of black metal stuck out of his wound. I attempted to remove it but it did not budge. I now realized Match was seriously wounded. I told Kelly I had to get to the 2nd Battalion. Kelly said he'd get Match a medic then he would catch up with me. I didn't say anything about Match's wound but I wondered if he would "make it." I did not see Harold Match again until 1975 at a reunion. He had with him the whole tail-fin assembly of a Japanese mortar that had been removed from his shoulder. He was fortunate to live through this.

I moved along the stream edge until I came to a bridge. I was now back near the beach I landed on earlier. I observed more Marines coming ashore under fire. The Japanese were dropping mortars on the Marines still on the beach. I crossed the bridge, but was pinned down with a half dozen 3rd Marines. After a short wait they moved and I moved toward the area assigned to our 2nd Battalion. I was aware of the tick, tick, tick sound of a Japanese Nambu machine gun as I ran for cover.

I decided to move across an open area when a mortar dropped behind me. I ran for the other side of the clearing when a mortar dropped in front of me. I doubled back realizing I was being singled out by a very good Japanese mortar man. I found a slight depression and laid still to catch my breath. Unexpectedly, Kelly dove in next to me. I related to Kelly the feeling I had about my personal Japanese tormentor and his accurate mortar. Apparently, Kelly was not convinced and we decided to make a break for the other side of the open space. As we ran Kelly told me he and another guy had hauled Match to the beach. I asked Kelly if he thought Match would live. Kelly expressed no opinion but merely shrugged. I am certain the lack of mortar fire as we ran convinced Kelly I was imagining my Japanese mortar man. A moment later a mortar landed behind us. I had to say, "You see Kelly - I wasn't dreaming." Kelly was impressed enough not to laugh at the premise again. We later laughed about our world record dash.

We pulled our line into their 2nd Battalion and hooked up our wire. We called our base camp to assure our line was still in. Our regimental H&S was at least hooked up to one of our firing batteries. The 2nd Battalion was still setting up their pack Howitzers and digging foxholes. We knew other members of our H&S wire teams were hooking up the 1st, 3rd, and 4th Battalions. With all the Japanese firing, we knew some of our guys would be hit.

Kelly and I headed back to our base camp. Upon our arrival, we learned our 2nd Battalion line was out. The mortar fire and trucks and tanks movements on the beach area assured us our lines were constantly under threat. We found the break just a few feet past the beach bridge. A quick splice and we had communications flowing. We attempted to move our wire lines to less traveled areas. The continuing Japanese fire and our troops moving off the beach kept our line in constant jeopardy. As we moved along a road just back of the beach we saw a number of dead Marines, Marines on stretchers, and walking wounded. The 3rd Marine Division hospital tent was just being set up. (This hospital sustained a direct mortar hit the first night and a number of wounded and medics were killed.)

Our wire fixing and replacing took a lot of our day. We stopped at our Division Headquarters to refill our canteens and talk with some communications men we knew from communications school days.

The day was about over, but we decided to do one more check of our lines before going back to our base camp.

We passed one of our cooks and another Marine sitting on the edge of a foxhole. I told them the location of our base camp, but our cook said he was going to stay put for the night. As we left they were opening "C" rations and obviously settling in for the night.

FIXIN' TO GET KILLED

Kelly and I realized it was late, but we had to check in on our 2nd Battalion line to make sure it was operating before we headed in for the night.

As we dove into a shell hole, during a particularly heavy mortar barrage, we almost jumped on Lieutenant Sharp of "L" Battery.

"You boys are fixin' to get killed running around out here," he suggested.

Kelly responded as only this Irishman could. "You're right, Lieutenant, but this is our routine. We merely splice wires and romp around. But that's why we get the big money."

Sharp smiled as he departed and said, "I guess you earn it."

I turned to the smiling Kelly and concluded, "You keep smarting off to the brass and we'll both see the brig."

Kelly replied, "Any brig would be better than this."

It was getting dark and we had better get back to our base camp. Movement on the beach was almost at a stand still as night closed in. Everyone had a foxhole to settle into for the night. In the storm of the day's events and the intensity of combat we hardly realized we had spent the entire day running, diving for cover or dodging trouble.

OUR FIRST NIGHT ON GUAM

We noticed only a few Marines were moving about. As we moved toward our base camp we talked very loud to assure no trigger happy, uptight Marine took a shot at us. Finally, we entered our base camp at the base of the low hills that surrounded the rice paddy. Our base camp was bedded down for the night and we agreed it was too late for us to dig a foxhole. Our machine gunner had set up a perimeter defense around the inland side of our camp. We entered from the beach side.

Kelly and I decided to spend the night in a dry irrigation ditch at the right flank of our base camp.

The Japanese were still dropping a few mortar round but even they seemed to be settling in for the night. The ships offshore had begun firing parachute flares that lit up the whole area with a dull, green light. They kept this up until morning to give some vision to the boys on the front lines. This also discouraged infiltrators from sneaking through our lines.

We hadn't been in our irrigation ditch very long before a loud talking shadowy figure joined us. My God, it was Colonel Wilson, commanding officer of the 12th Marine regiment. Kelly broke the silence, "Welcome to our elongated foxhole." The colonel replied "You boys must have been working late, also." The Colonel asked us if we had any water to spare. We both offered the Colonel a canteen and told of filling our canteens at the Division water trailer to assure the Colonel we had plenty of water. We had come ashore with two canteens of water, but we needed water to counter the extreme heat of Guam. The heat was a very debilitating factor during our fighting on this island. The Colonel expressed his appreciation for the water and asked our names. The Colonel knew us but it was so dark he couldn't see our faces.

As we laid in the ditch recounting the day's events, Kelly commented he hadn't eaten all day. Then, I remembered the meatloaf in my pack. I pulled the towel wrapped meatloaf from my pack. Our eyes had become accustomed to the dark and the flare shells permitted me to see the surprise on Kelly's face. I turned to Colonel Wilson and said "It's chow time - how about some meatloaf." The Colonel thought I was kidding and replied, "I would prefer steak or chicken." I offered the meatloaf and explained how I got it. This brought a chuckle from the Colonel and Kelly. I cut up the meatloaf with my K-Bar knife and the three of us ate it with a hunger driven by a hard day's work. We shared our water one more time and prepared for a long combat night.

At one point we saw a Marine machine gunner fire a few rounds from his position on the hill in front of our camp. The disclosed machine gunner promptly received the attention of a Japanese mortar. We knew that burst of fire may have cost that Marine his life. We also knew the only reason he would have fired at night was to stop a nearby Japanese infiltrator. This meant the Japanese were moving in. Not a comforting thought for us as the night dragged on.

"No! No!" Bang! The Colonel, Kelly, and I sat up at full alert. That rifle shot was in our camp and very close. Now there was a stir at the radio tent foxhole. Words were spoken. A cry for medic. Roberts, a radio man, had been shot by one of our own men. Roberts was taken to a tent not far from us where our regimental physician examined him. The Colonel asked for a report as soon as the doctor determined the extent of the wound. We heard the physician's report. The bullet had passed through the stomach to the lower bowel. Nothing could be done to save Roberts' life. Roberts left a wife and a newborn child he had never seen. The man who shot Roberts was immediately transferred out of our outfit.

This is a standard operating procedure (SOP) in cases of accidental killing.

The first night on Guam was far from restful.

In our irrigation ditch we all slept with one eye open. The Japanese helped us in this by dropping a round or two of mortar fire too close and too often. In combat we hated the nights and the days were seldom cakewalks. Night held too many unseen terrors, not the least of which was our overactive imagination. The parachute flares continued to cast an eerie albeit necessary light over our entire perimeter.

I asked Kelly if the rattling I heard was his beads (Rosary) or his knees shaking. Kelly replied "Shut up and pray." Kelly had a way with words.

DAYBREAK DAY 2

Finally daylight. Our camp began to stir. Gunfire increased all along the line. We knew our lines were being probed by the Japanese and we also were testing the Japanese lines.

Sergeant Love came by telling us to get up and square up (look alert.) Fortunately the Colonel was already in counsel with Colonels Letcher and Fairborn. I asked Sergeant Love what happened to his vocal "Reveille" that he employed on Bougainville. Love smiled and walked back into the camp. I could hear his deep bass voice saying "Reveille, Reveille." I can still hear it. Sergeant Love was shot and killed four days later. Another great loss.

Kelly and I were anxious to have a foxhole after our night exposed in the irrigation ditch. A deep foxhole I might add. Corporal Wyly and Bob "Iggy" Ignatius were stirring around their foxhole and pointed to a spot in front of their foxhole where there was room for Kelly and me to dig our hole. This placed us at the extreme front of our camp at the left flank just before the 6 to 8 foot drop off to the stream that edged our camp. We were reminded we were also the most forward in case of an attack. Very disquieting. We took heart in the fact the stream afforded us a bank of six to eight feet that any intruder would have to scale.

Our grousing about getting last choice of the foxhole locations was cut short by Charlie Presser telling us to get out on the broken 2nd Battalion line. In his infinite wisdom, he again suggested we get the lines into the trees and off the ground. We decided to run a new line and patch the old line if we could find it. The "if" was caused by tanks or trucks pulling the line until it was completely lost.

The Japanese were pelting our perimeter with artillery and mortars. We could tell the difference by their sound. The mortars sounded like "womp." The artillery like "thump." We could see the fresh results of the "womps" and "thumps." We saw the Division Hospital from a distance and some of our communications men from the Division told us how bad the direct hit had been.

We had taken our line along the edge of the stream bed and as we approached the beach we were able to get our new line up in some trees. We also saw the beach area had sustained a lot of Japanese attention during the night. As we moved toward 2nd Battalion we passed the foxhole occupied by Phillips, the cook, and his foxhole partner. Their hole had taken a direct hit by a Japanese shell. Both of the mangled bodies lay at the bottom of their foxhole. I had to reflect to Kelly, "If he had only been where he was supposed to be."

US Marine Corps 155mm rifle on White Beach (Agat Beachhead) being fired at 1,400 yard range. Taken by APA-1 USS Doyen. Prior to July 28, 1944.

FOXHOLE DELUXE

As we passed a tank, we saw a couple of tank men climb out of a foxhole dug under their tank. Wow- that had to be the grandest foxhole on the island - and safest. Some guys got all the breaks. Foxholes were our safest place but they were uncovered and subject to direct hits. A tank would provide the ideal cover. In combat, any bit of security was coveted.

We recrossed the beach bridge and things were relatively quiet. Then, the quiet became loud, and loud became louder, and louder became a roar. By the time we reached 2nd Battalion we were obviously in a major bombardment. We crouched on the beach area seeking any shelter available. At this point Corporal Wardlow and another Marine joined us. We all agreed that to attempt reaching the 2nd Battalion H & S under this heavy fire was asking to be killed. I approached one of the firing Batteries of 2nd Battalion and learned they had a line into the Battalion Headquarters. I called Captain Moss to tell him the situation at 2nd Battalion and that I could get a line by tying into the firing Battery switchboard. He agreed this was a good alternative and told me to get the Headquarters into our communication net by way of the firing Battery.

Just after I hung up on my call to Captain Moss, the Japanese mortar bombardment stopped. We were able to run the telephone line right into 2nd Battalion Head-quarters instead of the alternate plan I had cleared with Captain Moss.

Three Marines and their machine gun put a nest of Japanese snipers out of business. The fox hole was about 100 yards off the Guam beach. The Marines, left to right: Gunnery Sergeant J. Paget, Privates L.C. Whether and V.A. Sot (?) July 28, 1944.

A LITTLE CORNER OF THE WAR

As we left the 2nd Battalion and moved back to the beach, our attention was drawn to the high hills over-looking the beach. The Marines were attempting to beat back an enemy assault and retake the ridge of the hill. A company of the 3rd Marines would charge up over the ridge only to be driven back by heavy Japanese fire. They would come tumbling back down the hill dragging their wounded and dead with them. This life and death struggle went on for a half hour. After numerous unsuccessful attempts to gain the ridge, the Marines called for a heavy artillery barrage at the top of the hill. We watched this erupt at the ridge. A Navy Destroyer moved in close to shore and joined in the barrage at the top of the hill. When the artillery, mortar and ship-board barrage ended, the Marines made another assault and cleared the hill of its defenders. All of us watching this heroic stand cheered the Marines as they took the heavily defended hill. Corporal Wardlow shared the feeling I had when he said, "This sure beats any movie." Seldom in combat are you able to observe the type of battle we had just observed.

When I arrived back at our base camp, Captain Moss read me the riot act. If you recall, I told Captain Moss I was going to tie the telephone line into a firing Battery switchboard. Then the firing let up and I was able to go right to the 2nd Battalion Headquarters. My big mistake —I did not notify Captain Moss of my change of plans. I knew better and Captain Moss had made his point.

THE RAIN'S CAME

Another night and more problems. We had a big rainstorm and the creek just below our foxhole became a torrent. It floated some dead Japanese bodies and dead animals to just below our foxhole. The stench was unbelievable. Kelly and I were forced to stay in place until dawn. In an attempt to filter out the overpowering odor, we bunched our blankets against our face, but the stench was able to permeate through everything.

Then, as if this wasn't enough, we heard movement in front of us. (Recall we are at the outer perimeter of our camp.) Neither Kelly nor I had a hand grenade to toss at the movement. We asked Wyly and Ignatius if they had a grenade. No answer. Stage whispers weren't going to arouse Wyly or Iggy. Finally, we got their attention but they didn't have a grenade. We had boxes of grenades all over our camp, but now that we needed one, none were available.

We knew better than to fire our rifles at the noise so we sat in our foxhole expecting an assault at any minute. Earlier that day John Wyly had shot and killed an infiltrating Japanese soldier in this very creek, so we knew it was a way known to the enemy.

The night dragged on and we expected a Banzai attack at any moment. We were not disappointed in this fear.

BANZAI!!

With the dawn there was a marked increase in gunfire, mortar, and grenade explosions at the very edge of our Camp. (Perhaps 30 yards at our right flank.) Sitting on the left flank, I expected action at any moment. A fifty caliber machine gun of ours began firing a few yards to our left. I saw Colonel Letcher pointing up the hill directing the machine gun fire. The fire volume had increased to a constant staccato interspersed with multiple grenade and mortar explosions. There was no doubt our camp was involved in a major fire fight.

At this point, Lt. Rogers came to our foxhole and asked John Wyly to get four or five men and join him for a patrol on the hill over our camp. Wyly told Kelly and me to stay put with Bob Ignatius to hold this flank of our camp. Wyly grabbed Bob Wolfe, Harry Bailey, A.H. Rogers and joined Lt. Rogers. Kelly and I were backed up by a number of our communicators and we needed some hand grenades. I ran over to a pile of ammunition and grabbed a box of grenades. Just then Caesar Adami came back from the front with a bleeding head wound. It appeared to be mostly his ear. He said a bullet had ringed the inside of his helmet and nicked his ear as it exited his helmet. A superficial wound, but painful and bloody. As I dashed back with the grenades, Adami ran back to the area he had been defending when he was hit. Adami was dead moments later as he was shot through the stomach.

I could see Colonel Letcher at my left continuing to direct the 50-caliber machine gun ignoring Japanese mortar and small arms fire. A Japanese officer rose waving his sword to direct his men. Colonel Letcher directed the machine gun fire that cut the Japanese officer down. Colonel Letcher was an old man by our standards—but one hell of a Marine.

At one point they came for Kelly and I felt deserted. We saw movement in the tall weeds before our camp. I fired a few rounds at the movement in the grass. I knew it had to be a Japanese soldier, but after the movement I did not see him again. (We later saw his body not far from where I saw him move.)

Sergeant Presser called to me. The 4th Battalion line was out. While not my usual assignment, I took Maio and Seppi with me to troubleshoot the line. The entire front line was erupting and they needed all the artillery we could deliver. The three of us moved out onto the exposed rice paddy toward the 4th Battalion. Our line was strung on the stumps of decapitated trees. I had to climb up to the line that was tied to the tree with a "loop down" knot. The concept of this loop down knot was to facilitate a quick release of the line when one grabbed the loop down knot. The idea was you grabbed the loop of wire hanging down and the line was released. With the continuing fire from all sides of our perimeter, the thought of even a few seconds up a tree was disheartening. I tightened my pole climbing "hooks" and ran up that twenty-foot tree as fast as any human had ever climbed a tree. I grabbed the "loop down" and jumped back. Unfortunately the knot was not a "loop down." I dangled 10 feet off the ground. To extricate myself from this embarrassing and dangerous position, I had to swing out and reset the steel spikes of my climbers in the tree. I then had to cut the wire and jump down from my exposed position. I was on that tree for less than a minute but I felt I had been exposed and under fire for an hour. Maio, Seppi, and I laughed as we reflected on the presentation I made while dangling from the tree. Once again, we found reason to laugh even under the most dire conditions.

We repaired the wire and opened the communications to the 4th Battalion.

The Japanese offensive was still pressing from the hills and we remained exposed on the rice paddy. The formerly dry rice paddy was soft mud after the heavy rain. We passed through the firing batteries of the 4th Battalion. As we slogged along, some familiar faces of the "M" battery popped up to offer advice. "Hey Peterson, keep your ass down" and some saltier expressions.

We were now at the extreme right flank of our beach perimeter. Our 21st Marines were up in the hills over the rice paddy in an intensive firefight. I prayed they stayed the Japanese offensive because we were just below them. I had to wonder how Jack O'Keefe was faring up there.

We spotted the seaside houses that undoubtedly had been occupied by Japanese upper-echelon officers. We approached them cautiously, but found them vacant. Whiskey bottles and china dinner-service confirmed our impression that this had to be a residence of some of the Japanese high-command. We did not stay long at these houses fearing we were in a too-exposed location.

We made a hasty departure back to the rice paddy and on to our base camp. The firing had abated and we stopped at the 4th Battalion headquarters only long enough to assure our lines were still functioning.

AFTER THE STORM

As we entered our base camp, there were a number of poncho-covered bodies. All boys of our base camp.

Corporal Wyly had been seriously wounded and had been taken to the beach to be evacuated to a hospital ship. Lt. Rogers had been killed, but we were able to find his body. His death was confirmed when his jungle boot was found with this foot still in it. The medics had packed his toes and they recognized their packing. A group of suicide Japanese infiltrators had blown him up with a heavy explosive charge. Corporal Bill Coila had been shot through the arm. He was patched up and returned to duty.

From Bob Wolfe, A.H. Rogers, and Harry Bailey, we learned about Lt. Rogers' ill-fated patrol. The patrol led by Lt. Rogers proceeded up the hill above our base camp. The trail was blocked by a huge boulder. Lt. Rogers climbed over the boulder followed by John Wyly. On the other side of the boulder they were confronted by a number of Japanese infiltrators with large packs of explosives. A firefight ensued. An exploding grenade threw Wyly back over the boulder. Wyly was seriously wounded and bleeding from leg, body, and head wounds caused by the exploding grenade. Wyly ordered the patrol to fall back expecting a greater explosion from the Japanese. Wolfe refused to leave Wyly who felt he could hold back the oncoming Japanese. It soon became obvious the Japanese patrol had retreated back. Wolfe sent A.H. Rogers back for a stretcher. Wyly was taken off the hill with no further trouble and taken to the beach for immediate transport to the hospital ship off shore. In 1945 we saw John Wyly back in San Diego and he related his side of this story.

COPING WITH DEATH, EVERY DAY

We had lost 8 killed in what later was called "The Last Banzai" (a book by Jack Kerins of our H and S 12th Marines.) I walked down the row of poncho-covered dead lifting the poncho to see the faces of our fallen comrades. I didn't have to do this, but felt obligated to say one last goodbye.

Kelly accompanied me on the tragic viewing. I turned to Kelly and said, "Boy, this is going to be rough on a lot of folks back home." Kelly nodded in agreement. Then I asked Kelly, "Hey do you know what we are having for chow?" The crassness of my departure from mourning our losses to "what's for chow" never occurred to me until days later Kelly commented on my callousness. I was apparently unaware of this cold response. I regretted having been seen so uncaring, but Kelly understood. This was a form of closure. Although appearing hard and cruel, it was how we coped and what made it possible to carry on and exist under these dire circumstances. What was past was past. We moved on and did not dwell on the morbid. We did not have the luxury of grieving. I tell you this to partially explain how we coped with death that was always so constant and near at hand.

BURIAL DETAIL

P.F.C Maio and P.F.C. Seppi had expressed an ambition to become morticians after the war. Unfortunately this post-war career-goal had been heard by too many. When our unit was asked to provide burial personnel, Seppi and Maio were tapped. When they returned from the cemetery they were obviously shaken and never again expressed a post-war career-goal.

THE MOVE OUT OF OUR GUAM BEACH PERIMETER

"Okay, let's move out! Grab your gear and move out."
We were breaking out of our perimeter at Asan Beach
and moving to a new combat arena on Guam. We
moved cautiously up the beach road to Agan, capital of
Guam. Past walled Chamaro cemeteries and then into
the ruins that were once residences of Agana. I strongly
suspect most of this ruin had been caused by our pre-
landing bombardment. We knew most of these residences had been housing for the Japanese. We stepped
off our light truck and proceeded cautiously through the
ruins. Our infantry had moved through these ruins
earlier but we knew a lone sniper could still be in them.
At the place I determined was the main town square,
there was a large building still standing. This appeared to
be the City Hall. Ominously, behind the large building,
was a huge round sea mine… and it was smoking!!

We knelt behind a wall and waited for the mine to
explode. After waiting a few minutes, we determined we
had to move on. As we departed the center of Agana,
the mine was still smoking. (We saw it a few days later
and it had not yet exploded.)

We rode up a road in back of Agana. At the top we set
up a temporary camp and awaited further word about
where we would eventually bivouac. Night came quickly
and we settled into the ruins of a frame house. We were

of the opinion our breakout had been accomplished with less problems and Japanese resistance than anticipated. As always, night brought the usual anxieties and realizing we were in an advanced position was a multiplying factor of fear. Some of our group had found a few bottles of Japanese Saki and were toasting the sunset or something equally foolish. Fortunately, there was just enough for a canteen cup to each celebrant and certainly not enough to impair my assessment of our front-line peril. As I mulled over our precarious position, a couple of "MP's" moved in beside our hovel and set up a machine gun post. Soon another MP showed up with a Doberman guard dog. Wow!! Our own private body guards. With that kind of protection of our front, five nearly sleepless nights behind me and a few gulps of rice wine (saki), I slept the best night's sleep since leaving the U.S.S Crescent City.

ANOTHER MOVE

The next morning Kelly, Crickmore, Jack Cooper, Wolfe, Devey, Lt. McGuire and I moved up to the Guam airstrip. We spent the day laying communications lines on trees or back off the road where necessary. We occupied a deserted frame house on the edge of the airfield. Laying lines to our firing batteries and forward observing positions called for us to cross the Guam airfield. The airfield was covered with destroyed Japanese aircraft. No

American planes had landed there yet. We moved very cautiously across the landing strip. This was an exposed expanse so we move sporadically to make as poor and unpredictable target as possible. Out on the airfield we found a large "Bay City" earth-moving-machine shovel.

Obviously, this had been captured by the Japanese and then used to improve the airport. We were very careful in our approach to examining the "Bay City" unit. It appeared a perfect item to booby trap. We cautiously opened the doors and tool chests, but found no booby traps. We found the Bay City ready to operate and no bombs attached. However, in front and in back of the "Bay City" shovel were neatly piled rocks about six inches high. Upon examination we were able to determine these little rock piles concealed the firing pin of a buried bomb. Had the "Bay City" been moved, it would have detonated the hidden bombs. Fortunately, the Japanese were too precise in concealing this booby trap.

We called to our Division Headquarters and they patched us through to our combat engineers. We stayed on guard until the engineers arrived. We watched them disarm 250-pound bombs and then they dug up the bomb. I had just found another job in the Marine Corps I was glad to see someone else perform.

The ever present summer heat took its toll and by nightfall we were ready to collapse. The press of combat needs did not permit rest periods or easing up.

In our frame house on the edge of the air strip, our evenings were spent getting a quick meal, watching the days dust and sweat, and making ready for another restless night.

In our organization, George Cooper was unique in that he never swore or used any form of invective. George was old by our standards and was in his mid to late twenties. Perhaps his maturity was indicative of his speech cleanliness.

Being housed near the front lines even extreme fatigue did not dull our apprehension or alertness to strange sounds. Any sound, movement or disturbance immediately brought us to full alert. We knew our survival depended on our wits. We had all just settled in for the night when we heard a loud buzzing caused by some large flies at one of our windows. Don Crickmore, ever a foil for George Cooper, asked, "Hey George, what are those flies doing?" After too long a silence George Cooper responded, "I think they are diddling!" The room erupted in an uncontrolled laughter. The ever present tenseness we all lived with, eased just a bit and humor won again.

We were always at full alert at dawn. We were expecting problems but were also elated the night was over. Our combat breakfasts were sparse. We heated water for coffee, consomme, or hot chocolate. Small compressed wafers of a flammable substance provided the heat. C-rations were eaten—but not relished. Back in our base camp, we would have powdered eggs, bread, coffee, peanut butter, apple butter, and orange marmalade. We also had "tropical butter" that was more like tasteless cheese. It had a high point for melting and was believed to be better in the tropics for not melting.

The food was consistently bad, but consumed and tolerated. We were expending so much energy we had to eat to keep up our strength.

A JAPANESE WAVE

After breakfast we were told our base camp was moving up and telephone lines had to be moved. I moved to the road that passed by our house and prepared to put on my climbing spurs. (We called them hooks.) Devey, Wolfe, Kelly, Maio, and Skutel were standing nearby preparing to join me. I was kneeling to tighten my climbers when I became aware of a clanking sound.

It was the noise of a Japanese tank traveling toward me on the road at high speed. I had seen Americans driving captured Japanese tanks in Agana and gave the tank little attention until it was a few feet from me. I waved at the guy standing in the tank's turret. He waved back as he passed. I jumped up and screamed to the other

Marines, "That was a Jap tank and that was a Jap running it!!"

Just after my warning the Jap tank stopped about 50 yards down the road. We all scattered. The Japanese tank turned right and climbed the embankment and drove across a field to a position about 100 yards behind our house. As we returned to the road, an American tank roared down the road. We waved at the tank to stop. We told the tanker the position of the Japanese tank. The American tanker closed his turret opening and drove up the embankment to meet the Japanese tank.

It took only one round from the American tank to reduce the Japanese tank into a blazing mass of junk with internal explosions. We wondered if the Japanese tank crew had escaped but subsequent examination of the burned out tank confirmed all had died in the tank.

This episode became one of the most talked about events of our entire operation. I think it was Devey who first asked me if I always waved at the Japanese. He certainly wasn't the last. Captain Verne Kennedy always kidded me about waving at the enemy. (Even after the war when we met again at the University of Michigan.) In quieter times reflecting on the incident, I centered on the fact that the Japanese tank commander purposely saved my life. Had he merely swerved his tank he would have crushed Devey and me. A short burst of his machine gun or pistol would also have finished us.

Instead, he smiled and waved. I can still see him and I continue to ponder his merciful act.

The Guam Campaign was winding down and we moved to our last combat base camp. In a few days our Marine and Army units were formed into a solid line of skirmishers across the entire island of Guam. We swept up the island seeking Japanese stragglers or snipers. Our infantry units were assisted by war dogs. As the line moved, we set up telephone checkpoints to coordinate this sweep. At one check point in front of the line of skirmishers, I was confronted by a war dog. I had left my rifle on the jeep and knew I'd never reach it before the "war dog" attacked. Then the animal bounded out of the brush and into another mess of foliage. It was a full grown deer and not the war dog I perceived. I breathed a sigh of relief.

OH, MISTER SAM!

"Oh, Mister Sam, Sam, my dear old uncle Sam. Won't you please come back to Guam?"

The Japanese were harsh taskmasters as conquerors of Guam.

They drove people out of their homes and into open fields. They were told these fields were now their place of residence. This was especially hard on the elderly. To cope, the Guamanians built lean-tos and other shelters.

Any expression of discontent was severely dealt with by the Japanese.

During the occupation of Guam by the Japanese, the natives lived under strict rules. The slightest error was severely punished by the Japanese authorities. Some islanders were even beheaded. In defiance of the Japanese, the Guamanians had this little ditty asking for Uncle Sam to return. If the Japanese heard the song, severe punishment was administered, even death.

GUAM, ISLAND BEAUTIFUL

Guam was by far the most beautiful island we were on while in the Pacific. The weather was pleasant although hot and tropical.

The Guamanians were very friendly and appreciative of our action to free their island. We took pride in the fact we were the first to liberate a part of the USA and these American citizens. As we reoccupied Guam, the civilians would come through our lines, elated at being freed, and singing this song. It was a catchy tune and the words, although contrived, were rendered enthusiastically and with love:

> Oh, Mister Sam, Sam, my dear old
> Uncle Sam
> Won't you please come back to Guam?

Fifteen destroyers, sixteen battleships
Coming and advancing never to retreat
Oh Mister Sam, Sam, my dear old
   Uncle Sam
Won't you please come back to Guam!

The Guamanians were so appreciative of their liberation. Their smiles and words of encouragement were a boost to our already soaring morale. To think we were able to save these lovely people.

Fifty years later in 1994 we were invited back to Guam for the anniversary of the liberation. The people were still open in their praise of our efforts. This was a great experience. As part of the "Liberation Day" festivities we were seated in a reviewing stand to watch the Liberation Day Parade. The rain soaked all the paraders but did not cool their enthusiasm. I fought back tears as 25 or 30 rain-drenched children faced our review stand and sang.

Oh Mister Sam, Sam, my dear old
   Uncle Sam
We are so glad you came back to Guam

A most moving moment.

STILL A PFC: A COMBAT MARINE IN WORLD WAR II

AUGUST 1944

The fighting on Guam was over. We moved to our permanent base camp at Ylig Bag across the island from Agana. Our camp was on a high hill with a breathtaking view of the Guam Coast.

We attended the dedication of the Asan Beach cemetery. I was designated a driver for Captain Moss, Lt. McGuire, and another officer. I had little experience in driving a jeep and the trip to the cemetery was memorable. At one point I careened off the roadside embankment and on another curve had the jeep on two wheels but eventually we made it to Asan Beach for the dedication. We sought out the crosses of fallen friends and paid our respects. (In 1994, we found the entire cemetery had been removed. All the bodies had been sent to their home cemeteries or if the family chose, the body was taken to a large military cemetery on Hawaii.)

The Commanding General of the 3rd Marine Division spoke words of praise for the dead. Taps were sounded. A very short, very final, farewell. The Marines obviously didn't linger over sad affairs.

LIEUTENANT CHARLES PRESSER

We learned one of our own was commissioned in the field. Our Sergeant Charles Presser stepped forth, sporting shiny gold bars of a Second Lieutenant. Well deserved recognition of a great Marine. The bad news was he would be transferred out of our H & S Battery.

THE SIMPLE LIFE

Our life in the Marine Corps was spartan and without many perks. Our food was poor, our tents were bare, and we had little in the way of entertainment. Added to this miserable milieu was the constant knowledge another battle was on the horizon. (Battles that took quantum leaps in their intensity -- they never got easier.)

Having pointed out some of our less favorable conditions, I must add life in the Marines was simple. Meals were served on time and announced by a bugle playing mess call. Mail was distributed after the proper bugle call. "I've got a letter, I've got a letter, maybe you have got one too."

All our bugle calls had been verbalized over countless years of soldiers responding to the blare. Pay call sounded out and we knew "Payday, payday, whatcha going to do with a drunken sailor?"

The point I wish to make, is that our life was simplified. We were called to eat, we were summoned to get our mail, even payday was reduced to responding to a bugle call. We were lined up for medical shots; we even were put to bed by taps and awakened the next morning by sickening renditions of "reveille." Unfortunately, as I have mentioned before, our bugle players were so bad it was hard to determine what they were attempting to play.

I never longed for a life as a bugle-responding soldier. However, I can recall as I returned to civilian life, and the need to handle all of one's needs, made the days of simply responding to a bugle not seem at all intolerable.

Then, strangely in combat, we were often on our own. We had tasks to perform but we had little supervision. We ate when we could find time and we slept when we could, and our officers and NCOs left us alone to complete our given rounds. Our task was to keep our communication lines functioning and it was accepted we knew our job and we were left to do it. The big rub came in heavy-combat periods. We were expected to do our job even at risk of life and limb.

Because of the demands of our specialty, we were not burdened with mess duty, guard duty, or other scut work. I think there was a belief this balanced out the dire side of our combat experience.

PEACEFUL ROUTING

Out of combat George Cooper, Kelly and I were the camp electricians. In this role, we set up our electric lines, hooked up and maintained the generator, and handled any shorts or outages that occurred. Our generator was an ancient number and we powered it with an even older Hudson Motor car engine. Very frail—but it provided us with the power necessary for our Headquarters Battery.

On one occasion we started up the Hudson Motor but when we threw the lever to activate the generator the whole operation ground to a halt. This indicated we had a major short on our lines.

As we passed Colonel Wilson's tent he called me over to tell me he needed lights as soon as possible. I told Colonel Wilson we were all working on the problems and we hoped to find the short soon. The Colonel had just turned to return to his tent when Kelly hollered he had found the short. The Colonel turned and asked Kelly if it would take long to fix. Kelly in his own direct manner responded, "Hell no, Colonel. Some dumb son of a bitch has wrapped a wire over both the hot and neutral line."

Unfortunately the dumb SOB was a lieutenant standing in the tent and the Colonel saw him flinch. As the Colonel walked away I saw his shoulders shaking from laughter. He said to me over his shoulders, "Peterson, my compliments to Kelly." I am certain Kelly had made the Colonel's day. Colonel Wilson's days were numbered as our commanding officer. He was promoted to Brigadier General and Colonel Crist took his place.

DENGUE FEVER

As we settled into our new camp on Guam, we were hit by Dengue Fever. We attributed this outbreak to the clouds of house flies and mosquitoes we were experiencing.

Dengue Fever is a particularly nasty malady. Extremely high temperatures, vomiting, and diarrhea for days on end. I personally had a temperature in excess of 107 degrees. The medics told us such temperatures could only be tolerated in the tropics. I do not recall any fatalities, but recall extreme weight loss among sufferers. Frankie Mayo lost so much weight I walked by him before I did a double take and exclaimed "Mayo, you're skinny!" Fortunately the Navy sprayed the entire island of Guam with D.D.T. This ended the housefly and mosquito plague and the Dengue Fever outbreak.

The battle of Guam was over and we settled into a familiar routine. Cleaning gear, rifles, clothing and awaiting inspections.

A HAIRY INSPECTION

"Alright, you jar heads. We fall out for a General's inspection at 1300 hours." (1:00 pm) Bad Bad News! I had just washed my hair and I hadn't had a haircut in four months. My hair grew thick and fast and it looked like a scared afro. Our camp barber Dave Bethany was already swamped.

What to do? As I readied myself for the inspection, I felt if we stood the inspection covered (with helmet on) I might just skinny by. We fell in (assembled) at 1300 hours and the General, my God it's General Wilson, was there promptly at 1315 hours. We knew Colonel Wilson had made General but this came as a complete surprise. As the General moved up and down the ranks, he made friendly comments to the older members of our battery. Then it happened!

When he was three or four men down from me he turned to the accompanying Major and Lieutenant and said "Have the men uncover." The Top Sergeant responded and as I removed my helmet, I felt my hair rise to the occasion and stand straight up. I stood, helmet in hand, and every hair on my head at attention. The snicker from the ranks behind me was less than comforting. Then there stood General Wilson staring directly at my abundance of hair. Very stiffly he commented "a little bushy, isn't it Peterson?" as he passed on. The Lieutenant asked me my name. The General turned and told the Lieutenant "That won't be necessary - he's one of my boys. I owe him for dinner the first night on this island." The General moved on after a final smile.

After this incident, everyone wanted to know what I did

for the General the first night on Guam. Kelly told of sharing the meatloaf.

BASEBALL AND OTHER GOOD STUFF

Our 12th Marine Regiment had a baseball team—as did the Division Headquarters. We had games between other regiments and also Army and Navy teams. These ball players played a superior game of ball. Many of our players held major league contracts and others had played on minor league teams.

The Championship game was held on our ball field between the 12th Marines and the 3rd Marine Division Headquarters Team.

Our pitcher was Don Crickmore backed up by our catcher George Cooper and Centerfielder Charlie Root. (His uncle was the Chicago Cubs star pitcher.) There was Buddy Rich, later a famous jazz drummer, from 3rd Marine Division HQ, and the rest of the team has melted into time.

We were being readied for another campaign and this meant shots for all hands. The baseball team was given a reprieve until after the game to assure only the spectators had sore arms.

That noon as I stood in line for lunch, a big mouth Sergeant boasted that the Division Team would beat our home team into the ground. Irate, I suggested the Sergeant put his money where his mouth was.

He snapped back, "I've got fifty bucks sez the Division wins." Speaking faster than thinking I said, "You got a bet," so I accepted the Sergeant's offer.

Now -- if I had fifty dollars this would have been a poor bet against the favored team. However, since I didn't have thirty cents, the bet was maniacal.

To save you the pain I experienced during a close ball-game, let me tell you I won the bet. I also learned a lesson. The weight of the fifty-dollar bet was so heavy, I didn't enjoy the game that I had looked forward to for months. Money cannot make up for lost happiness or enjoyment.

As we were returning from Iwo Jima, I ran across the catcher for the Division baseball team. We knew he had a contract with the St. Louis Cardinals. Unfortunately, he had lost both his feet on Iwo Jima.

ROBERT APPLEBAUM - ONCE A MARINE - NEVER A CIVILIAN

There were Marines that loved the Corps and Marines that detested the Corps, and Marines that really hated the Corps and there was Robert Applebaum who carried the loathing of the Corps to new levels of repugnance.

Bob charged into our tent on Guam in a very irate condition. He stood in the middle of our tent and proclaimed, "I hate the Marine Corps. I hate the Officers. I hate the Colonel. I hate the Sergeants and I hate you, because you are a member of the Marine Corps." We all understood Bob's position statement on the Marine Corps because he had expressed it before at the least provocation and on many occasions. Perhaps, you can understand my surprise when I learned recently that he had retired from the Marines after 30 years active duty. He fought the battles of World War II, Korea, and Vietnam. Seem they just don't build hate like they used to.

OKAY O'KEEFE

Jack O'Keefe showed up at our camp soon after the fighting was over. His 21st Marines had taken heavy casualties but he came through unscathed. We shared news from home and reminisced about days we spent in Chicago that now seemed eons ago. For a few days, the living was easy and the war remote.

Then Jack O'Keefe was off on field exercises. At H & S 12th Marines we worked on equipment and received new equipment. We trained and exercised. We had the feeling we would be on the move again. We noticed our mail was newer. We were issued the ominous two cans of beer. We intensified training; fired our rifles; and the sure sign - medical shots were administered to all hands. Strangely, even the rear-echelon staff were given the full issue of shots (tetanus, bubonic plague, typhus.) We realized we were getting close to Japan and knew by the intensity of recent combat and Japanese ferocity that this next campaign promised to be a world beater. Summed up in a few words, "They never get easier."

A NEW WRINKLE

We were told the next combat area had a particularly deadly snake. To ensure our safety, we were ordered to soak our wool blankets in a nasty smelling solution. After this ablution, the blankets were dried—but retained a strong kerosene odor. We presumed the snakes were repelled by this petroleum aroma because no one was bitten. I must add, we never saw a snake.

Shot and shell weren't enough. Now we had to look out for snakes.

As usual, once the wheels started turning and they plied us with the two beers and sped up our mail, lavished medical shots on us, it always ended with us aboard a ship and a new beach on the horizon.

I guess I was never really ready for "the next combat landing." We knew it was inevitable, but we accepted it as our lot in the Marines. The signs of pending action was now very clear to us; faster mail, two cans of beer and the shower of medical shots, and oh yes, an inspection of our "dog tags" (two medical identification tags with name and serial number and blood type.)

At the last minute, Harry "Mayor" Kelly was deemed unfit for combat by the medics. He had an unexplained red rash on his back.

My foxhole partner on Guadalcanal, Bougainville, and Guam was not going to be with me. A bad omen. And at this time, we read the "omens" all too clearly.

As we departed for our ship, Kelly handed me his pistol and said, "Pete, bring it back to me!"

IWO JIMA

This ship was a Merchant Marine ship. After a couple of days out of Guam, we were told we would be floating reserves for the 4th and 5th Marine Divisions in assault on an Island named Iwo Jima. I recall standing on deck as we were approaching this new operation wondering if this Iwo Jima would become famous like Guadalcanal. We stood off an island we were told was Chichi Jima. We were told the 4th and 5th Marine Division would hit the beach on Iwo Jima the next morning.

Our radios told us Iwo Jima was being shelled by a huge fleet of surface vessels and being bombed by waves of bombers. We were assured this had been in process for over a week. The next morning we stood off a miserable gray island with a modest dormant volcano at one end. It was not a large island, but we knew if we had committed two Marine Divisions and another in reserve this must represent a specifically-defended piece of real estate. We did not expect a cakewalk.

Noticeably absent from this campaign was talk that all the shelling and bombing meant the assault would be easy with light casualties. We knew the shelling and bombing was necessary—but seldom accomplished the softening up they were meant to accomplish. Replacing rosy predictions was the more cynical, "They don't get any easier." We no longer dreamed of an easy touch.

Map of Iwo Jima detailing the invasion.

THE BATTLE FOR IWO JIMA

The first wave reached the beach with relative ease. The the reports from the first waves on the beach became grim. The entire front was pinned down by withering and accurate Japanese fire. Small arms, mortars, light and heavy artillery. The reports indicated the Japanese apparently had the whole island "registered in" for their guns and cannons. (If one can imagine the entire battle-field divided into a grid of small squares. Then realize at any given time the Japanese could drop a mortar shell or artillery shell or both into any of these squares. You can understand the concept of having the "whole island registered.") This fact, plus the advantage of looking down from Mount Suribachi on to this registered grid, gave the Japanese a great advantage over our initial assault waves. The Japanese took full advantage of this accurate-fire capability.

The reports went from bad to worse. The reports had this unit pinned down and taking heavy casualties and then another unit expressed the same deadly dilemma. The beaches were jam-packed with troops and material and they were all being systemically chopped up by accurate and heavy Japanese fire. High surf and Japanese fire had littered the beach with broken and destroyed landing craft. The soft black volcanic sand bogged down the tanks on the beach. The beaches were clogged. A few Marines made it inland a short way in face of every type of explosive ordinance.

From our offshore position the entire landing area appeared to be under exploding fire. Dust and smoke obliterated our view. The American planes were pounding Suribachi. We saw some of our planes crash into the ocean. One S.B.D (Dive Bomber) was in trouble. The rear gunner bailed out—but his chute did not open and he fell into the sea. The pilot pancaked into the ocean, stepped out on the wing of his downed plane and was picked up by a destroyer. We saw no rescue of the tail gunner.

The reports from the beach never improved. Each foot gained was taken at a high price in dead or wounded Marines. This was shaping up to be a deadly operation and we knew we were destined to be committed. The second day continued bad.

The 4th Marine Division had fought its way across the narrow neck of Iwo Jima dividing the Japanese forces in two. The 28th Marine Regiment was forming up to assault Suribachi while the 5th Division moved against the main part of the island.

Tracked landing vehicles (LVTs), jam-packed with 4th Marine Division troops, approach the Line of Departure at H-hour on D-day. In the center rear can be seen the control vessels which attempted to maintain order in the landing.

COMMITTED

The word we had been expecting came on the third day, in the form of an order. The 21st, 9th, and 12th Marine Regiments would commit immediately to support the Marines on Iwo Jima. The 3rd Marine Regiment would remain as floating reserves (the 3rd Marine regiment was never committed and this action caused General Holland Smith a lot of post-campaign criticism.)

Amphibious assault on Iwo Jima, a DR-8 wire communications reel is at left-center.

GROUND ZERO

Our landing on Iwo Jima was as traumatic as we expected. Hundreds of dead Marines were poncho-covered awaiting burial. Constant mortar fire and small arms kept us crouched or prone. As in all combat areas, there was the smell of rotting flesh. The stretcher bearers carried wounded to landing craft for evacuation to awaiting, sparkling-white hospital ships. The gleaming white ships with huge red-crosses painted on their sides stood out among the gray naval vessels that continued to shell the island.

Marines burrow in the volcanic sand on the beach of Iwo Jima, as their comrades unload supplies and equipment from landing vessels despite the heavy rain of artillery fire from enemy positions on Mount Suribachi in the background.

There appeared to be an endless line of walking wounded and the dazed individuals with vacant stares and trembling hands. This is the reality of combat. People get hurt - people get killed.

Gear and material was piled everywhere. Those unloading supply boats moved fast and not systemically. The need for quickness was necessary lest they be hit by Japanese fire. The result was a jungle of jumbled equipment, ammunition, and vehicles. Out of this mess, we understood the beach captains could locate any needed item. If true, it would be a miracle.

Captain Moss ordered me to get as much telephone wire as possible. There was a sentry on the telephone equipment as on other equipment on the beach. (It was widely known a good Marine never came up short on equipment.) My problem now was to get wire past that sentry. I told the guys with me to be sure to address me as "Sir" or "Mr. Peterson." I had a safety pin I pushed through the back of my dungaree blouse to show only as a silver pin in my lapel. (In combat, officers pinned their insignia out of sight but the small pin sliver showing was sufficient to establish them as officers.)

I stormed up to the the sentry and in the most arrogant manner announced "Private, I want my men to get as much of that wire as possible to carry!" His only response was "Yes, sir." My detail of men would have loved to laugh. I would have liked to think I carried the day with my officer-like demeanor. My detail of men overdid the "sir" talk all the way to our camp. They expressed the opinion that the 45-automatic on my belt; binoculars around my neck; dispatch case over my shoulder; and my dumb face was more the reason I was accepted as an officer. That makes sense.

We moved to our base camp just behind the 1st airstrip, Motoyama #1. The routine was much the same as the first days on Bougainville and Guam. The intensity of fire the first days on Guam and Iwo Jima were very comparable, however on Iwo Jima this intense fire never abated. We fanned out from our headquarters switchboard to our firing batteries. The distances on Iwo Jima were shorter. Everything was crowded and compact. Our beach head at this point was not very large. I ran into Hum and Norman heading for a forward observation post (they would spend 4 days there before being relieved.) They both made it without injury.

Out of the gaping mouths of Coast Guard and Navy Landing Craft, rose the great flow of invasion supplies to the blackened sands of Iwo Jima, a few hours after the Marines had wrested their foothold on the vital island.

THE SORDID, DEADLY

We were in a very difficult situation. To move was a death defying act. To stay in one place allowed a sniper or mortar to zero in on you. This dilemma haunted us, but we had others depending on our completing our assigned role in this hellish arena. Rather dramatic, but we moved from one hole to another hole. You got the feeling you were more into the island than on it. Thank God for shell holes.

As we arrived at our Second Battalion, the firing batteries were digging in their gun. The communications men we talked to wanted to know what was happening up front.

The situation was tenuous, but our lines held and advanced slowly.

The 21st and 9th Marines (Infantry) had moved into the front lines between the 4th Marine Division and the 5th Marine Division. The 12th Marines (artillery) was set up and functioning.

On a plateau just off the Iwo beachhead, Marines dig in for protection against enemy fire and the heavy rains. Barely visible in the background is Mount Suribachi.

A VIEW OF IWO JIMA

As I moved around Iwo Jima, I saw a study in grim. The ground was grey. The little remaining vegetation was grey and broken and the sky was grey. The dust had painted the trucks, guns and equipment grey. You can see by my evaluation this was an unpleasant place. We lived in constant threat of Japanese mortars, artillery, rocket, and small arms fire. The most terrifying, to me, was the ever-possible deadly sniper. A swift, deadly, unexpected shot held one in a grip of terror. Yet, we carried on and lived under these conditions. Another heart-stopper were artillery air bursts. (Japanese anti-aircraft guns depressed to fire exploding shells a few feet overhead.)

Over all this grey and fear was the stench of death. Humans and animals killed by the shot and shell of combat decompose very rapidly and hang a cloud of rotting flesh over the entire warring arena. We had this stench on Bougainville and Guam, but it isn't something you can get used to.

The near and far sounds of war keep you ever alert, yes on edge. The lack of sleep dulls one's senses, but you remain alert for any extraordinary sound or movement. Days are an eon of time, nights are an eternity.

The endless lines of wounded being moved back for evacuation reminds you of the danger ever present.

Smoke and dust still obscure most of the landscape, rising from the phase of fighting that overran this Jap position on Iwo Jima. A Marine takes a look at the anti-aircraft, dual mount, weapon captured from the enemy.

There was another big problem for me. My foxhole partner Mayor Kelly was not with me on Iwo Jima. My new foxhole partner would be George Cooper.

When I returned to our base camp, some of the guys pointed out the land of our camp was dimpled where mortars had exploded. Mortars exploded upon hitting the ground and the explosion leaves a small shallow dent in the ground. Our camp was covered with these mortar dents. It was disturbing to dig a foxhole where mortars had already had occasion to hit.

Another thing added to my personal discomfort. As I

mentioned above "Mayor" Kelly was not with me. My new foxhole partner George Cooper of "diddling" fame. As we settled into our foxhole for the first night, I noticed Cooper, a known Catholic, was not rattling his rosary beads. I called this misplay to Cooper's attention. He responded he didn't even have a rosary with him. Though upset, I had to admit I hadn't asked Cooper about his religious beliefs before I chose him for a foxhole partner. Seems George's mother had gone to church "every day of her life" and died a terrible death from cancer. This had soured George on religion. I did not make any future reference to Cooper's agnosticism but it did give me a lot of concern those nights on Iwo Jima.

The 3rd, 4th, and 5th Marine Divisions moved slowly up the island. We were elated Suribachi was taken. Then our attention focused on Mt. Suribachi as the marines atop the volcano put up a small American flag. Everyone on our side of the front cheered. It was a moving moment. It was a little flag, but it meant we no longer had to expect fire from two directions. What a sight seeing our flag flying over Suribachi was. This flag raising was not the more famous photographed flag raising on Mt. Suribachi.

From the crest of Mount Suribachi, the Stars and Stripes wave in triumph over Iwo Jima after U.S. Marines had fought their way inch by inch up its steep lava-encrusted slopes.

We know this flag raising and the second (more famous) flag raising irked the Japanese because they greeted these events with heavy mortar and artillery fire. This was a day we would all remember. Incidentally, during active combat the flag is never lowered. It flies 24 hours a day.

The Japanese fire power was evident on Iwo Jima. Their heavy artillery drove off a transport that rounded Suribachi. We were pounded by mortar, artillery, and small arms fire. They had a large rocket that became sort of a laughing matter. They would launch the rocket, but it was not very accurate. It would soar over the island, past Suribachi and out into the Pacific Ocean. Because of the crowded conditions on our beach head, had the large rockets fallen into our area, many lives would be lost. One large rocket or spigot mortar landed in an ammunition dump and caused a major fire and loss of lives.

One of our Sergeants brought a new man and asked me to take him out and show him how we maintained our telephone lines in a combat area. We departed our camp and after about ten minutes came under a heavy mortar and artillery barrage. My companion and I dove into a large shell hole. I carried on a monologue conversation with my green recruit while he caught his breath and guts. I could see he was in his first barrage and he had every right to be terrified. I told him he was fortunate to be in the 12th Marines H & S. I told him he would see no stripes of promotions but we had a great group of guys. He said he didn't care - he was a Tech sergeant and didn't need any more. He told me he got a stripe for each school he completed.

Yep, I was irked. He stayed in the States and got the promotions. The boys in combat got zip. Seemed counter to the Marine concept of being a Marine. This experience may have had long term effects on me. When asked if I was going back to college, I would always reply, "Yes, I've had enough of life, as a private."

While the green Marine (also around the gills) and I clutched the side of our hole, a stretcher team on the road came under heavy fire. When they realized the barrage was coming toward them they dropped the stretchers and all fell flat on the ground. When the barrage lifted they resumed their trek to the beach. I mention this episode, because I have seen films of it. At the time I did not realize a combat cameraman was watching it also.

Our infantry units continued to sustain heavy losses. The 21st Marines casualties were at 10% (eventually some units were over 120% casualties. Replacements allowed these casualties of over 100%.) The 9th Marines were in the same condition. Yet we kept moving up the island. The 3rd Marine Division was assigned the center sector with the 5th Division on our left flank and the 4th Marine Division on our right flank.

Earlier I mentioned our 3rd Marine Regiment was not committed to the Iwo Jima campaign. General Holland Smith has been roundly criticized for holding this seasoned combat regiment aboard ship in floating reserve and committing green untrained Marines to these extremely harsh battle conditions. Many of these youngsters had only been in the Marines for a few months and had no combat experience. The results were predictable—heavy losses and a large number of combat fatigue cases. In defense of General Smith, it is axiomatic in military books that the last reserves are not committed unless the campaign is collapsing.

We had a number of "Condition Red" alerts on Iwo Jima. We also had a "Condition Black" (counter invasions) but nothing came of it. We expected paratroopers or worse. We cleaned our rifles, checked our store of ammo, sat up on alert most of the night and all for naught. Naught in such cases was good!

As I have noted before, being a telephone lineman afforded us the unique advantage of moving all over the island. On one occasion, I ran into a Chicago friend Walter "Peanuts" Bennet. He was in the 5th Marine Division and we had our talk in a Japanese concrete bunker. (I envied him in his safe haven.) He brought me up to date on things and people back home. I told him Jack O'Keefe was on Iwo Jima with the 21st Marines. Peanuts knew about the 21st and his only response was, "Ouch!" (Peanuts made it back home in one piece.)

A SEARCH FOR PRIVATE O'KEEFE

My concern for Jack O'Keefe was even greater after my visit with Peanuts Bennet. I went up to the front lines to see if the 21st Marines could give me some information about him or perhaps get a chance to see Jack. I realized the 21st Marines had been hit hard and I was very apprehensive about Jack's life.

At the 21st Marines Headquarters I expressed my concerns to a Sergeant in charge. He told me O'Keefe's outfit was in a very advanced position and he did not recommend it as a place to visit. He added they did not have an O'Keefe listed as dead. I took some comfort in that.

A Marine flame throwing tank, also known as a "Ronson", scorches a Japanese strongpoint. The eight M4A3 Shermans equipped with the Navy Mark 1 flamethrower proved to be the most valuable weapons systems on Iwo Jima.

FAST & LOW

Moving back to our base camp, I passed two Marines crouched beside a wrecked vehicle. They suggested I move "fast and low" over the hill crest ahead of me. They said the Japanese had a very accurate 47 mm anti tank gun and had been using it to snipe at individuals or anything that moved. I will assure you I moved "fast and low" (near the speed of sound.)

I returned to our base camp frustrated in my efforts to locate O'Keefe. Compounding the problem, I had a letter from my mother asking me to tell Jack to write home. Jack's mother had called to tell my mother she was worried about Jack (as well she should be.)

That night the Japanese dropped a large mortar or rocket on an ammunition dump between us and Suribachi. This provided us with an unscheduled fireworks display as exploding ammunition lit up our area. This took a number of Marine lives.

(There were ammo dumps all over the rear area. An errant shot by the Japanese had a chance of causing a major explosion.)

Symbolic of the power and muscle that finally wrenched Iwo Jima from the grasp of the Japs, are the Marines who push their Jeep forward through the sand when the machine failed to make headway by its' own power.

SPEEDY HUNGRY

A couple of rocket firing trucks set up immediately behind our camp. The launching rockets were very noisy and the wailing sound added something new to the cacophony of combat noises. On one occasion a Japanese artillery shell scored a direct hit on one of these rocket trucks. The resulting explosion hurled unexploded rockets over a wide area. One of the unexploded rockets fell into the foxhole of "Hungry" Robins. We heard a new world's record was set for evacuating a foxhole under fire. The story of "Speedy Hungry" was told and retold.

In this horrible hell-like atmosphere of complete warfare, it always amazed me how we found humor and had occasions to laugh. Under such stress, funny or unexpected incidents were magnified.

An example of this happened a few days before Hungry Robins' race to fame. One of our PFC's showed up for breakfast with a very red face. This had been caused by a mortar landing on the edge of his foxhole and the flash from the explosion singed his face. We laughed uncontrollably at this near deadly incident. A red face, was after all, a red face.

At our base camp, a sniper's bullet kicked up dirt over our heads. We heard the rifle fire and went immediately to where we were certain the sniper was located but could find no sign of the Japanese. This was the nature of the war on Iwo Jima. We had no safe area. We knew the Japanese sniper had emerged from one of many tunnels they had dug under Iwo Jima. This labyrinth of tunnels and passages gave the Japanese access to many parts of Iwo Jima. These unexpected sorties from the tunnels kept us constantly on alert.

*HILL 362A on Iwo Jima looking at top and north face.
Dotted lines indicate the underground Japanese tunnel system.
One of five sketches prepared by the 31st U.S. Naval
Construction Battalion.*

The battle of Iwo Jima pressed on. Advances were measured in yards. The casualties mounted. The Japanese gave little sign of quitting and the Marines were giving more than they were taking. Our lines were now more than half way up the island.

One morning we began taking incoming mortar from a different direction. Incoming rounds make a whomping sound. We know this sound well. It was determined the mortars were being fired from two very small offshore islets. The Japanese had obviously occupied these islets overnight. Our 12th Marine artillery immediately fired on the island and scored numerous direct hits. A Navy dive bomber had also been directed to the islet and scored a direct hit with a huge bomb. We suffered no further mortar rounds from the islet. The islet appeared to have been broken in two.

AN ECHO FROM THE PAST

I was checking some lines to one of our firing Batteries in a rear area of Iwo. I had just been up front looking for Jack O'Keefe and was convinced any news about Jack would be bad. Preoccupied, I failed to notice my accuser.

"Hey Peedeesin. Do you think you'll ever make a wart on a good Marine's ass?"

I was startled out of my thoughts by a familiar voice.

"Hey Top!" It was Sergeant "Top" Warner of "blow it out" fame. This was a big surprise because I knew Warner had been sent Stateside after Bougainville.

"Sit down, Peedeesin and tell me about my boys in "M" Battery."

"Top, I just saw Hum and Norman a few days ago heading for an FOP (Forward Observing Post.) I'm no longer in "M" Battery. I'm in H&S 12th."

"Yeah, I signed your transfer when we were on the 'Canal.'"

"Well, Sarge, M Battery got hit pretty hard on Guam. Lucas was hit on the first day and a dozen others. Iwo's been tough, so there will be more bad news."

"You made it OK so far?" Warner asked.

"Yea, Top, scared as hell, but I've made it clean. Too many snipers and mortars on this rock."

"Peedeesin," the Top Sergeant's Louisiana accent murdered my name, "I signed your transfer out of M Batter to get you away from Bowman and a Sergeant who had you in his sights. You needed a change or you'd be in big trouble."

I looked at the smiling "Top" Warner. He had just explained why I was transferred out of the M Battery. I had thought it was just luck.

"Top, you did that for me?" I contemplated the old Sergeant in a new light. I had always thought of him as a cold uncaring Marine clod.

"Yeah, you're a good ole boy, Peedeesin. You just needed a break."

At this point, I sat down next to my new found friend and shared the wheel of a 155 Howitzer. Obviously, a friend I never knew.

"Peedeesin, stay live. After Iwo, you should be sent Stateside."

"Sarge, I've heard that rumor since Bougainville. I

expect to be in the FMF (Fleet Marine Force) Pacific for the duration."

"Keep your nose clean. It could happen."

"Hey, Top, three years in this lashup and still a PFC. How clean can you stay?"

"Boy, you deserve better but the Corps is slow to promote."

"Top, you made my day. Good seeing you. I've got to run. They don't pay me for sitting around jawing with an old retread like you."

"Peedeesin, how you talk! I was just beginning to like you. Stay alive and give my best to the boys."

As I walked down the road after this chance meeting with Warner, Iwo Jima seemed a bit better. The old Top Sergeant had really cared. How about that?

PLANE EXCITEMENT

The island seemed to be abuzz with a report that a disabled B-29 bomber was limping toward Iwo Jima after a raid on Tokyo. I climbed to the top of Motoyama #1 airfield to get into a better position to observe this landing. Realizing this plane could also crash, I took a position next to a Japanese one-man foxhole lined with a 55-gallon drum. All eyes were on the approaching plane.

Would it make it to the strip or fall short? We all held our breath as this huge plane gracefully settled on to the landing strip right over my head. A cheer went up all over the island like the cheer that accompanied the flag raising on Mt. Suribachi.

Moments after the plane landed, we experienced another response from the Japanese mortars and artillery. The let us know they also had seen the plane land. I jumped into the Japanese-styled firing pit. As safe a place as available as the Japanese vented their anger. When things quieted down, I was able to get a close-up inspection of the disabled B-29. We had never seen the monstrous plane up close. The crew expressed their elation to be on dry ground and were quick to express appreciation for the tough battle that made the landing possible. We had been told how important it was to obtain a place to save crippled air crews and here was the first proof of this. (Before the war's end, 5,000 such landings were made on Iwo Jima.)

ANYONE FOR TOKYO

On the way to Iwo Jima, I had made the acquaintance with a news correspondent from the Chicago Sun Times. We played poker and on one occasion, I loaned him money to stay in the game. He was interested in my activities because I was from Chicago. Toward the end of the Iwo Campaign he showed up at our camp to tell me he was going on the first night fighter flight over Tokyo. He asked me if I'd like to join him on this flight. I wasn't sure this was a legitimate offer, but I was not interested in getting myself any more involved in the war than I was already. He laughed and said he understood. I told him I never wanted to put myself in a position where people could lament my demise by observing "had he only kept his nose clean, he would have been alright."

I would define "keep one's nose clean" as not asking for trouble. (You may recall I felt the same way on Guadalcanal when we had the opportunity to fly as machine gunners on raids over Rabaul.) I also applied this lifesaver to souvenir hunting. We knew the Japs booby trapped souvenirs and I didn't feel the junk was worth the risk. So you see, "keeping one's nose clean" was a way of life and way to live.

To summarize this "don't ask for it" attitude: an assigned duty or an assignment given by someone in authority did not fit into the don't ask for it category. It was only an extra elective-activity one chose to do.

One of our souvenir hunters found all the Japanese medical records, which indicated our pre-landing barrage and bombardment caused very few casualties. The Japanese had deep bunkers and stayed in them out of harm's way.

THE RETURN FROM TOKYO

When my Chicago Sun Times correspondent returned from the night fighter flight over Tokyo, he reported he could see the fires of Tokyo a hundred miles away. He also reported the trip was uneventful—but scary.

THE WINDING DOWN

The battle for Iwo Jima was nearing its end. The remaining organized Japanese resistance was in a small pocket at the extreme end of the island. Sporadic sniper incidents occurred, but we knew it was all but over. We felt great relief that the killing was ending and before long we would be heading back to Guam. We had not been told we would be heading back to Guam, but dreams of going stateside had been foiled so many times we now expected a more plausible probability.

As we neared the end of this campaign, a new fear quietly arose. "Be careful - don't be the last one killed." We felt this haunting thought on the final days of Bougainville and Guam also.

We knew Iwo Jima has been declared "secured" quite a time ago but we awaited the final word. ("Secure" meant victory was assured even though some fighting continued.)

ANOTHER DIRTY SECRET

We landed on Iwo Jima February 22, 1945 and departed six weeks later. During this time we were given two containers of water a day to drink -- and bathe. We soon learned bathing in a quart of water took planning and speed. None of us perfected this and the results were obvious and odorous. We did have clean faces and clean vital body parts (required by order of Commanding General.) Fortunately, the Commanding General never checked on this.

A SUPER MOVIE

One evening we were told a movie would be shown. Another sign Iwo was history. The movie was "Saratoga Trunk." We all agreed this was the greatest film we had ever seen. I strongly suspect the message carried by the film (Iwo was over) clouded our appraisal of this film.

AN ANGEL IN DUNGAREES

Her name was Morton. Not particularly pretty woman but certainly pleasant. She was a Nurse on an ambulance plane sitting on Motoyama #1 airfield. She worked very methodically on the wounded. She had a smile and word of encouragement to each wounded Marine. I merely stared. She was the first woman I had seen in 18 months. (The betel-nut chewing natives of Guadalcanal and native Guamanians excepted!)

THAT LONG AWAITED MOMENT

"All right you Marines. Saddle up. Look sharp. We are going to the beach to board those landing crafts. Anyone who wants to stay on Iwo make it known to the Top Sergeant." (A taste of Sergeant's humor.) The tone of the Sergeant's voice betrayed his own elation. The Sergeant continued "We are going to board the landing crafts with the eyes of the Army, Navy, Air Force and civilians on us. We just won a big one and lost a lot of good men. Let your pride be reflected to these onlookers. Fall in, attention, forward march, route step march."

Those words never sounded better. We were leaving Iwo, we made it, we were alive and unscathed. O Happy Day!!

Yes, the most happy day! We boarded the landing craft pushed up against that black sand that had run red with American's blood only a few weeks ago. We looked back at the gray land, the brown-gray volcano, this piece of hell that claimed so many American and Japanese lives. I felt if I never see this place again it would be to my joy. It was a place with no pleasant memories.

One other blessing. We never saw the deadly snakes we

had soaked our blankets to repel. We suspected someone overreacted.

The landing craft pulled up the ramp and it was a form of closure. One door closed we knew the next door had to be better.

We moved to an awaiting transport ship with the ever-present landing—net hanging over the side. The wave-tossed landing-craft pressed against the ship and we took our turn scrambling up the side. The pitch of the ship made climbing the landing net more difficult—banging our bodies and hands against the ships side. However, this was not the time to gripe. We made it! We are unhurt! We are alive! What a day! What a great day!

As I neared the top of the net, a familiar face called to me. "Hey Peterson, get a load of this." It was Al Miller who waved to the mid ship and over the loudspeakers I heard Bunny Berigan's "I Can't Get Started With You." I can't remember hugging Al Miller, but he certainly warranted a warm embrace. This great day in my life just kept building.

THE DEMANDS OF THE IMMEDIATE

During the periods of active combat, I always enjoyed good health and was able to do my assigned job.

However, shortly after the end of the fighting, I would

fall victim to flu-like symptoms. Had this happened once or twice, I would dismiss it as chance, but it happened like clockwork after the end of each combat period.

I always felt the demands and stress of the combat period buoyed up my immune system until I had time to be sick. Hardly a scientific assumption, but it held true for me.

I expressed this observation to Dr. Anderson during one of the bouts with the flu. He confirmed that during combat he found his sick call were people with real hurts and fewer imagined maladies. I had the impression he felt the malingerers were too busy to employ their imaginations.

BACK TO GUAM

Our trip aboard this merchant-marine vessel became a comedy of errors. The ships crane off-loaded a huge bulldozer, the cable snapped, the dozer and the awaiting LCT (Landing Craft Tank) went into the ocean bottom off Iwo Jima. On the way to Guam, a large life-raft was lost over the side. In Agat Harbor, Guam, we almost ran down a Navy Destroyer.

Yes, it was back to Guam. Back to our old camp at Ylig Bay. Kelly greeted us and was apparently over the strange malady. We were back to a routine of lousy food, cleaning gear, and a dull existence. After Iwo, dull was good.

Safe at last. If you live under constant fear for a number of months, the glory of not having to worry is a balm of mighty power.

Wow! A disturbing thought. Actually, a constant thought. I am back to Guam and not a word from Jack O'Keefe. I'll soon have to write to Mr. & Mrs O'Keefe and relate the bad news. I rationalize he could be in a hospital or on a hospital ship. Or -- a lot of wishful thinking. I've got to write, but I'll wait a few more days.

I was walking to mess when who rounded the corner of our tent street but Jack O'Keefe. Jack could see how happy I was to see him. He smiled and said he had just gotten out of the hospital. He related being next to a wall on Iwo when a large shell landed on the other side of the wall toppling it over on him. He was pinned under the wall the better part of a day before someone heard his calling. He was exceedingly lucky. The 21st Marines sustained over 120% casualties but Jack survived. The luck of the Irish!

THE BIG TIPPER

Jack O'Keefe and I had the opportunity to go to a large Navy PX (Post Exchange.) Once there, Jack asked me if I had any money he could borrow. I gave him a twenty-dollar bill. We each purchased a package of cigarettes for 5 cents. As we walked away from the PX, Jack started patting his pockets obviously looking for something. Jack determined he hadn't picked up his change after tendering the $20 bill for the 5-cent purchase. I could not imagine not getting his change. How could he leave

$19.95, his change after getting his cigarettes? I suggested we quickly return to the PX and retrieve the $19.95. Certainly the clerks would recall such an error. Jack never broke step as we walked away from the PX and quietly said, "Forget it. I'm trying to establish myself as a big tipper on Guam!" We laughed all the way back to our 3rd Marine Division area. Life was so good!

GOOD NEWS AND BETTY HUTTON

We were all elated to learn a USO troupe was on Guam and was scheduled to come to our camp. The star of this group was Betty Hutton, singer, dancer, and movie star. Wow! The 3rd Marine Division was abuzz over the pending show.

Unfortunately, I was on duty as keeper of the electric generator and I viewed the show a city block away from the stage.

The entire performance was top flight and warmly greeted by the audience. Betty Hutton ignited the audience and she responded to the sincere response of the Marines. The crowd brought her back for an excited encore.

After her last curtain call, she entered the stage to thank the audience. She then called for a drum roll and asked all the Marines with three combat landings to stand.

Then, very quietly, she said, "What I am about to tell you is official from your Commanding General." She then jumped up and down and screamed, "Good News! You're going home!!"

There was a moment of contemplative silence as the meaning came to the standing Marines.

Then an explosive cheer from the standing, dancing Marines. The band kept playing "Happy Day" over and over again.

It was time! The long-dreamed-of-event. The Marines with three combat landings were going stateside. The applause and cheering grew. Betty Hutton's eye makeup smeared with tears. She danced and waved to the dancing, applauding Marines.

What a great performance and what an unbelievable gift to the audience!

GOING HOME!

It was going to happen! We now had official word. Those of us with three campaigns were going to be rotated back to the States. By God, we made it!

For years we have dreamed of this and now it is coming to pass. Life could not be better.

Mike Heinzman came into our tent and asked me if I was going to take the test for Officer Candidate School. I replied to Mike that we had tried for OCS on three former occasions and had not made it. I told Mike I was now headed home and did not want to be delayed a moment.

A few days later, Mike came to tell me he had been accepted for Officer's Candidate School and would be sent to OCS as soon as possible. (He spent four more months of Guam awaiting his call to OCS. The war ended and he never went to OCS. Life can be so cruel.)

We boarded a transport in Guam's Apra Harbor. The ship was a Coast Guard vessel the USS Fremont headed for the states for refitting. We were welcomed aboard as Iwo Jima heroes. We had the run of the ship.

As we left Guam's Harbor, we passed a submarine heading to Guam. They proudly displayed a broom (yes, a kitchen broom) on the conning tower indicating their voyage had made a clean sweep.

As the submarine passed the loud speaker on the submarine blared forth, "Ahoy, we salute the Marine heroes from Iwo Jima you have aboard. Well done and a happy voyage home." Then the flag was dipped aboard the submarine. Our ship replied "We are proud to have the Iwo Marines aboard and accept your salute and acknowledge your successful voyage indicated by the broom you fly. Godspeed."

The spontaneous salute from the Navy submarine made us all feel good and that our efforts on Iwo were appreciated.

Guam dropped out of sight and it was our last landfall until we hit Hawaii 4,000 miles away.

Life on the ship was boring. (After Iwo a lot of boring could be enjoyed.) We knew each day brought us closer to home. I noticed we now talked of "home" not "stateside." We stayed up most of the night reliving our days on the "Canal," Bougainville, Guam and Iwo Jima. New Zealand was something that had happened eons ago. We all speculated what we would do when we got home.

Many anticipated marriage to the girl they left behind. I had no girl waiting. My highschool girlfriend had sent me the infamous "Dear John" letter. This too, had passed away and I had few thoughts about her. In my response to her "Dear John" letter, I told her I hoped all her kids were acrobats. I sort of regretted this.

We also reflected on the guys we had left behind on Bougainville, Guam, and Iwo Jima. They too had dreamed of a trip to their home.

We also thought of the guys we left on Guam awaiting the next campaign. We were confident of defeating Japan but knew we would have to invade the homeland. We wondered if we would be back in the Pacific for those final battles. We knew our stint in the States would be short and then we would be shipping out again. Wait a minute!!! That is too far in the future. The present future is home!

While aboard, the Fremont we were told of President Roosevelt's death. This saddened us, because he was our President and he had served so long.

We were told we would be in Hawaii in a couple of

days. We continued our routine of staying up late, drinking coffee and listening to the ship's library of music.

The most popular, or at least the most-played was Louis Prima's "Robin Hood:"

> *Many long years ago a fellow named*
>> *Robin Hood*
> *Stole from the rich most every chance he could*
> *Then he'd scamper through the forest to the Blue*
>> *Boar Inn.*

Hearing Louis Prima gargle out this tale night after night for two weeks taught me these words that I still remember.

> *First there was Little John, then there was Alan*
>> *Dale,*
> *140 more together they would hit the trail.*

(Amazing what a few weeks of repetition can accomplish!)

YOUTH MUST ALSO SERVE

"Hey Pete, I just noticed. Today is my birthday."

"Jack A., how nice to be on your way home on your

birthday. Your folks don't know it yet, but you'll be home for a big time in Texas."

"Pete, I keep pinching myself. It is hard to believe it is true. Home again."

"By the way, Jack old man, how old are you?"

The skinny Texan smiled and hesitated to answer.

"Come on, I know you're young. What difference can it make?"

"Pete, I'm sixteen today."

"My God, Jack. You went overseas at thirteen?"

"Yep and I have been scared as hell someone would find out."

I promised Jack A. I'd not disclose his age. I reflected I had always considered Jack a good Marine. He did look young, but so did all our guys. Thirteen, how about that!

HAWAII

We quietly pulled into Pearl Harbor. We passed the sunken ships still in place since December 7. We docked at a pier overlooking a busy thoroughfare. No one was permitted off the ship. We were told our stay would be brief. A day and a half later we departed Pearl for the States.

THE STATES

More reading, card playing, coffee drinking, Robin
Hood and lovely boredom. Then San Diego, Stateside,
Marine Base, Home. We landed at the same pier we
departed from on the Bloemfountaine over two years
ago. What a day!

We were bussed to the Marine Corps base and as we
entered the base, the guards at the gates saluted and
shouted "Welcome Home." People standing at the gate
applauded. We were being welcomed home as Marines
among Marines. We were something special to the
Corps. As we progressed to the processing center, we
passed Marines Recruit Platoons drilling as we had on
the Marine Base Parade Ground. As we passed, the
Marine Drill Instructors ordered "eye's right" and again
saluted us. Certainly a far cry from the bus ride three
years earlier when all we heard was "You'll be sorry!"

At the "processing center" we were issued new uniforms
and our old greens (forest green wool uniforms) were
cleaned and pressed. These uniforms had been at the
bottom of our sea bag since New Zealand.

We were told a special banquet was being prepared for
us as soon as we settled in and showered. (Actually we
were very clean Marines. We showered two of three
times a day aboard ship to pass the time.)

We were ushered into a decorated mess hall. The menu was steak, fried chicken, seafood, fresh vegetables, and two or three kinds of potatoes, salad and every other necessity to make this a great feast. However, the hit of the day was fresh milk. Something we hadn't had since leaving the States. We gorged on milk and ice cream.

The Marine Corps Base Commander thanked us for our efforts overseas and told us the Marine base was ours until we left on furlough. He assured us our processing was moving ahead apace and we could all expect to be home soon. This was accompanied by wild applause. Our cup runneth over!

THE SARGE!

I went to the base barber shop intending to get the full treatment (the works.) Had to sharpen up for the home folks. As I entered, an old Marine in the first barber chair greeted me. "Hi Marine! Just back?" I replied, "Sarge, we just got back and I'm feeling great!" The Sarge asked if I was on Iwo. I told him I was on Iwo too long. He laughed and as he stood up the barber removed the barber sheet and there stood a two-star Marine General. Every Marine in the shop cam to attention. As he shook my hand, I told him I regretted thinking him a Sergeant and calling him Sarge. He said, "At ease, Marine. I must say being called "Sarge" is the highest compliment I expect to receive." We laughed and he said he was always proud to meet a real Marine. I was in too much shock to ask the General his name. One of the barber-shop patrons thought his name was General Arthur.

After the barber worked his wonders on me, I went to the base slopshute (beer garden) to see some of the guys from the 12th Marines. Unexpectedly, Corporal John Wyly appeared. You will recall John was seriously wounded on Guam during the Japanese Banzai attack. John was still in rehabilitation but looked strong and healthy. We filled him in on Guam and Iwo. He told us about his adventure aboard the hospital ship.

JOHN WYLY ON THE USS COMFORT

John related how he was bounced around on his way to the hospital ship. He felt no pain because of the morphine shot given him by our medics. He recalled the boat ride to the hospital ship. Then he found himself in an operating area. He noticed some Marines came out of the operating room missing a leg or an arm. He realized he may be facing an amputation. He attempted to tell the Navy Corpsman he did not want any limb to be amputated. Before he could complete his plea, an ether cone was placed over his face ending his conversation.

When John awoke, he was confused and it took some time before he realized where he was and what had happened. Then came the realization that an amputa-tion could have happened to him. With his eyes closed, he clenched his fist and assured himself he had his hands and arms. Then he wiggled his feet and they were there. He was very relieved. Then, from the dark recesses of his mind he recalled reading that amputees have feeling when a limb is actually gone. He now knew he had to open his eyes and eyeball his feet and hands. He chose to lift his hands first. He opened his eyes and the hands stood before him. Now, one more eyeballing remained. He lifted both feet at once. They were both there! There had been no amputation. John said he gave a great sigh of relief and went back to sleep for 12 more hours. After this experience of worrying about amputation, John said he experienced some pain, but nothing like those moments he feared loss of an arm or leg.

It was great seeing Wyly. He told us he had seen Harold Match and he was on the mend. Wyly told us Match had a whole tail-fin assembly of a mortar taken from his back. You may recall I attempted to pull a piece from Match's back, but it wouldn't budge. I obviously was pulling on the tip of this large piece embedded in Match's back. He was certainly lucky to live after such an injury.

This had been another great day with Wyly. It was good seeing him looking his handsome self.

The processing continued. We were given our pay, our

next assignment was determined, and we were issued tickets for our train ride back home. We were asked if we wanted to be stationed on the East Coast or West Coast. I opted for the East Coast and was assigned to the Opa Locka Naval Air Station, Opa Locka, Florida, a suburb of Miami, Florida.

HOSPITALIZED

Our departure was now eminent and I came down with flu-like symptoms. I reported to the hospital hoping for a fast cure. What I got was a hospital bed after a corpsman took my temperature. I was also given a couple of aspirin and told the doctor would see me in the morning.

Early the next morning I was awakened by a young Marine. He asked me if I had been on Iwo. I answered him and he began telling me he couldn't get over the experience. He told me of the black sand ridges and then there would be another ridge, and another. Never an end to the deadly ridges. As he related this with mounting terror, I could see he was well on his way to cracking up. I grabbed him and said, "Hold it, get a hold of yourself. It's over. You're back in the states. Don't let this get to you. You have to put the experiences behind you." He quieted down but I knew he was in trouble.

When the doctor showed up, he was a middle-aged Commander. He asked me how I felt. I told him better than last night, but my main object was to be well enough for my furlough.

The doctor quietly counseled me "It doesn't work that way. You stay until we say you go." I pleaded, "Doc, I've been overseas for two years and I need to get home."

The doctor did a double-take at me and inquired, "You're just back from overseas? What are you doing here? This is a recruit depot sick bay." I replied, "The processing center was next to the Recruit Depot and I went to the nearest medical facility to get something for my flu-like symptoms and ended up bedded down." At this point, we were both laughing at me being treated like a recruit. He offered to send me to the base hospital or for a car to take me to the Processing Center. I told him I'd rather walk. He told me my temperature was normal and that I should take it easy until I left the base.

As an after thought, I told the doctor about the Iwo Marine that was having mental problems over the bloody ridges of Iwo Jima. I could see the Iwo Marine sitting on his bunk and I pointed him out to the physician. The friendly doctor walked out to the ward desk with me and told me my cracking up Iwo Marine had been in the Marine Corps for three weeks. He was going to be given a medical discharge because he suffered from grand delusions and had no grasp on reality.

We shared another laugh and I left the hospital shaking my head. That kid had really snowed me.

As I donned my new forest-green uniform, I was given a small yellow striped ribbon (1.5"x.5") with three small bronze stars attached. These indicated I had served in the Pacific Theater of operation and had participated in three battles (one star for each battle.) While on Guadalcanal, we had served under combat conditions but this obviously didn't warrant a star. The Marine Corps was very chincy about giving out stars. (Seems riding a boat on to a beach under fire was the accepted criterion for a star. I must admit I did not seek another star.)

While I am talking about uniforms, let me tell you about the Marine Corps most recognized uniform - the "Blues."

THE "BLUES" BLUES

The most recognized uniform of the Marine Corps is the high collared, dark-blue coat and red-striped light blue pants and black cap with a white cover. Known in the Marine Corps lingo as simply "Blues."

Alas, I never had a set of "Blues." I was issued a forest-green uniform, very dull, very precise, but hardly in the same class as the "Blues." It was war-time and only a few postings called for a display of color. The "seagoing" Marines (those stationed aboard navy ships), the fortunate few assigned to diplomatic service at foreign Legations and embassies, and the White House contingent were issued "Blues."

As I see Marines on parade today sporting their Blues, I realize what could have been. Then I smile and gratify myself by realizing these blue-clad marchers would rather be able to bear my title of "Combat Marine."

HOME

Finally, I was on my way home. The train was a troop train with spartan accommodations but I enjoyed every minute of it. Each minute brought me closer to home. At each station stop, volunteers met our train with doughnuts and coffee. It was America at its best. It was also great being treated to their love of the service man. We pulled into the Lasalle Street station and a porter grabbed my sea bag and deposited it on the street in front of the station. He refused my proffered tip and moved away saying, "Welcome home, Marine." I wanted to get the feel of Chicago, so I boarded a streetcar instead of the faster cab. I was told by the "trolley Pilot" (aka conductor) I rode free. Chicago was extending itself. Chicago saw me coming. I was given free cab rides, free meals, free drinks, and admitted free to movies and sporting events.

I walked two blocks to my home from the trolley tracks

with my sea bag propped on my shoulder. Home from the sea. Strangers smiled and greeted me. I had the world on a string.

Post-war PFC Eugene H Peterson with parents, Signe and Hilding

When I came home, I expected an entire family to greet me but only my dad was home. My mother and sister were working in defense plants, but would be home soon. My dad reminded me that there was a war on. It was great seeing my dad and anticipating my mother, sister and brother coming in. My brother Richard was eight years old and a big fan of "Gene the Marine." As Dad and I reminisced, I prayed that he didn't start crying because if he did, I knew I would bawl like a baby. I was so happy to be home. My mother arrived with hugs and kisses. My sister Muriel also had hugs and kisses. Now the tears of joy.

Then Mrs. Rodkin just happened by and she was reduced to tears of joy, also. Then Mrs. Hornberger and daughter Jeanne came storming in to see their favorite Marine. Billy and Bobby Bitters, Jeanne Hornberger Bitters' sons, came in from school to see "Gene the Marine." Seems Gene the Marine was almost as one word, especially for the kids. Mrs. Hornberger won the biggest-hugger gold-medal. Then the relatives arrived and most of the population of the south side of Chicago. Yep, I was home and the homecoming was all I expected it to be.

I took an early break to run over to see the O'Keefe family. I had to tell them all about Jack, Guadalcanal, Guam, and Iwo. Jack's sisters were beside themselves over the good news. A lot more hugs. It was great being the bearer of good news.

During my May/June furlough, the only guys home with me were Edward Von Hermann and Jimmy Fawcett. We were all in the service and on furlough or special leave.

Jimmy Fawcett was in town for the funeral of his father, James "Red" Fawcett, aka James Foresight, aka etc. etc. Jim's dad had been gunned down by "persons or person unknown" as reported in the Chicago Tribune.

Eddy Von Hermann was in town to settle his father's estate. We had a number of good times but the high point was an evening at the "Pump Room" of the Ambassador East Hotel in Chicago. Eddy's sister Suzy suggested we get a date for Eddy and all go to the

"Pump Room" for an evening of dining and dancing. Sounded good to me. As we arrived at the Pump Room, I was greeted by a huge white starched-shirt asking if we had made a reservation. Eddy responded he did not need reservations at the Pump Room. The white starched-shirt swelled as Eddy stepped past me to confront the starched-shirt named "Henri of the Pump Room."

As he made his move he slapped the starched shirt in the stomach with the back of his hand and simply said, "Hi Hank, I know you will have a table for this Von Hermann and sister Suzy." Henri gaped at Eddy and when he could catch his breath, "My God, Eddy. I didn't recognize you in uniform (sailor suit.) Of course, we always have a table for you."

Henri signaled for a waiter and then expressed his regrets that Eddy was not able to be at the funeral of Eddy's father. As he spoke, he directed the waiter to make room for a table for this honored guests. To make room, tables had to be moved and a new table placed in a prime position. The patrons of the restaurant paid great attention to the table being set and waited the entrance of some celebrities that could commend such a stir at the staid Pump Room.

As we entered, an unranked seaman in the Navy and a Private in the Marines, the patrons -- especially the Majors and Colonels in attendance that had their table moved -- all stared. In point of fact, we were a Marine Private and a Navy Seaman and party who had an "in" with Henri the Maitre De. Henri wanted us to have the best of everything and if we ordered it he would make sure it was to our liking. We started with a glass of wine that Henri assured us was his best.

When he learned I had been overseas, he asked me what I had dreamed of. I said, Roast Beef. Henri said "No problem." (Recall this was a time of rationing and short-ages.) I told Henri I wanted Roquefort cheese on my salad. Henri asked me if I would permit him to make his famous Caesar Salad. We all agreed to the Caesar Salad.

Before long, Henri had moved to a table next to ours and prepared to make the Caesar Salad in a huge wooden bowl. He chopped a strange kind of lettuce, almost filling the bowl and then worked on the dressing. I hoped he knew what he was doing because he was making enough salad for the 12th Marine Regiment. After completing his wizardry on the dressing, he served everyone at our table, then passed the leftovers around the room doling our Caesar Salad to the appreciative patrons, saying compliments of the Messrs. Peterson and Von Herman.

For the rest of the evening people came by our table to introduce themselves and thank us for sharing our salad. We knew they were dying to ask us why we were treated so royally at the exclusive Pump Room.

Henri wanted to pick up the check, but Eddy insisted we would pay. What did we pay for a fabulous meal, fine wine, and an evening of dancing to a large band? Our total check was $32.00 and we left a generous $4.00 tip. At the time, this was such an enormous amount I hesitated to tell my Marine friend fearing they would think me a liar.

SENTIMENTAL JOURNEY

On my furlough, I had the opportunity to see people and places I dreamed about while in the Pacific. I even saw the girl that sent me the "Dear John" letter. My time in Chicago was all I expected it to be. But alas, it came to an end and I boarded a train (Flagler Flyer) for Miami, Florida and my new station.

The train ride was a three-day party. The Marines had provided a berth for me but I told the conductor to give it to some woman traveling with children and I was given a chair in the club car for the swap. The radio kept playing Les Brown's "Sentimental Journey," and this was truly a sentimental journey for me. To this day I think of that train trip when I hear "Sentimental Journey."

OPA LOCKA NAVAL AIR STATION

Opa Locka Naval Air Station was a flurry of activity. The station included two air strips, Naval Barracks, Marine Barracks and Wave Barracks. I soon learned my role was to be a guard and MP at this base and occasionally in Downtown Miami. This was a classic peasant becoming a king role. We were afforded many perks given only to people with arrest powers. Cooks would bring us their choicest foods to our posts, we were welcome at the officers club and watched the staff water down the liquor. PX personnel provided us with free meals and laundry service. All this to a group of guys that didn't have anything for three years. We never gave the moral issues in these freebies a thought. This was probably because no one asked us for special favors in return for gifts.

The Food on the base was excellent. Surprisingly, the food in the enlisted mess was better than the officers mess or officers club.

We had preferred posts on the base. The lonely Bomb Dump and deserted radio-station were spooky and time passed very slow. The main gates and Wave Barracks were preferred.

Fortunately Sergeant Moore (numero uno) liked Hyer and me. (We had both made three campaigns against the Japanese.) Because of Sergeant Moore's favor, we were always on the Main Gate or Terrance Barracks (Wave Barracks.) We also cemented our place in Sergeant Moore's heart when I gave a ticket to Colonel Prine, our Marine Commanding Officer, for running a stop sign.

We always enjoyed our time at the Wave Barracks. Their housing, Terrance Barracks, was a huge mansion reportedly built by Al Capone. The girls always had time to talk with us which helped pass the time. The women were just kids and very sweet. We seldom had any trouble with these Waves. In my opinion, these service women were the sweetest, cleanest and best behaved group of women I have known. I make this comparison against high school, college sorority and business women.

Having just sung the praises of this virtuous group I must relate a humorous incident involving a Wave. A Wave passed through the main gate carrying her hat. Regulations made it mandatory to be in uniform to go off base. As she passed, I casually said, "Square away that hat, Sailor." She kept walking and was outside the gate. I said, "Hey Sailor, square away that hat." She said, "I'm off the base and you haven't a damn thing to say to me." The group of sailors, Waves and marines looked for my response.

I stepped to her side and said, "My general orders give me authority within sight and hearing of my post. And you are going back on the base and your shore leave is cancelled." She stormed back on the base. On the base we exchanged words and the incident culminated when she hit me on my pith helmet with her purse. This didn't hurt, but it drove my helmet over my ears. I must have been something to behold because the Marines serving with me laughed at my appearance as I attempted to extricate my head from the helmet. The Marines on the gate asked what I intended to do to the girl who had just gotten the best of me. I told them nothing.

I explained she was very upset but if I reported the incident to officialdom, hitting an MP on duty would be a big beef. The mad Wave came by a few days later to thank me for not putting her on report. Her name was Ellen and every time she left the station after that, she would give me a big smile and shift her hat to assure me it was squared away.

Most of the sailors and waves were very young as I reported before. Just kids away from home for the first time. One evening, a young wave came on the base bearing her assignment papers from boot camp. She was in tears and said she just wanted to be home. She was so upset, I asked her to have a seat in the gatehouse. I told her "You tears aren't going to make a hit with your fellow Waves. These girls you meet at the barracks will be lifelong friends."

She finally got her tears under control. I told her she was so special on this base we provided a car to chauffeur her to her barracks. I called the Officer of the Day and requested a car. The homesick Wave looked out of the car and with a weak smile said "and you Marines are supposed to be so tough. Thank you for being so kind." She obviously reported this to her mother, because in a few days I received a nice note and homemade cookies. Strangely, I never saw this Wave again. She must have been transferred to another base.

PFC Eugene H Peterson pictured center

THE GLASS BOTTLE BAR

As I have related, we enjoyed our relationship with the Waves of Terrace Barracks. We were soon on a first name basis with many of those girls and invited to their local hangout, the Glass Bottle Bar, or as the Waves said, the "GBB."

One problem both male and female service personnel suffered was lack of money. Our monthly $52.00 (less insurance, etc.) did not allow us much room for opulence.

As we joined the celebrants at the GBB, we were warmly greeted. Being near destitute was not a real problem. If one had a dollar, it meant 10 beers for the group. On the center table was a money pool. If you had anything to contribute, you merely added to the pool. If you were broke, everyone understood.

Another source of income for the pool came from the establishment's slot machines. We were aware these crafty machines had a timing mechanism that allowed the unwary to win a small amount on the first dime or nickel as a promise of future returns. We waited patiently for 15 minutes after the last player of the machines and then reaped the 4 or 5 nickels or dimes. The bounty was then turned over to the pool.

I recall being very comfortable in the presence of these girls. There was little room for pretentiousness.

SOMEONE SPECIAL

My girlfriend was a Coast Guard Spar named Barbara Schultz. I met Barbara at the Orange Bowl Stadium during a high school football game. She was an ambulance driver. This gave her almost free rein over a Coast Guard ambulance. We toured around Miami and as far as Fort Lauderdale by Coast Guard ambulance. These were great days. Barbara Schultz was a lot of fun. She had a smile for everyone and was always ready to steal the scene.

On one occasion, she pulled up to the main gate at Opa Locka Naval Air Station. I was on duty and she stuck her head out of the ambulance window and in a voice loud enough for the crowd waiting for the Miami bus to hear, said, "Hey, Marine, how about a kiss?" The crowd cheered. Jim Hyer on post with me jumped forward and said, "Me too!"

I surprised Barbara by replying very sternly, "Sailor, are you here on official business?" Then, received the proffered kiss.

Our friendship continued after the war. She even spent one summer waiting tables at my folks' restaurant. I regret I do not know where Barbara is today.

Hyer and I got a 72-hour pass when Hyer saluted a retired Army Colonel in civilian clothes. Hyer checked his ID and when he learned he was a retired Army Colonel, he saluted him. It just so happened the Colonel was a close friend of Opa Locka Naval Station Commanding Officer. We were called to the Captain's Office, thanked for Hyer's military courtesy and given a 72-hour pass for our respect of the retiree. Sergeant Moore ate this up. We could do no wrong!

SERGEANT "IGGY" IGNATOVICH, SUPER MARINE

While at Opa Locka Naval Air Station (NAS) the entire station fell out (assembled) for Saturday inspection and review. At these affairs, any honors or medals were given out to the honorees. It seemed that Sergeant Ignatovich would be honored for bravery each week for his exploits while in combat.

One of his medals was for single-handedly fighting off Japanese infiltrators on Guam. "Although unarmed" the citation read, "Sergeant Ignatovich accosted the three armed-Japanese. Took the rifle away from one, clubbed one, and bayoneted another. The other fled into the woods." I think he was awarded the silver star for this action and keeping the Japanese from assaulting his company.

The next week Sergeant Ignatovich was cited for heroic

efforts on Iwo Jima. When his entire machine gun platoon was wiped out, Sergeant Ignatovich moved from machine gun to machine gun to give the Japanese the impression the ridge was well-defended and fully manned. During these exploits, Sergeant Ignatovich had a finger shot off. He bound his wound and continued his efforts until relieved in the morning. He was awarded the Navy Cross for this exploit (2nd only to the congressional Medal of Honor.)

What we have here is Sergeant Ignatovich, one tough Marine.

FREE ADVICE

Iggy came by my post at the Main Gate in his Jeep as Sergeant of the Guard. He seemed upset and preoccupied. I asked him why the frown? He replied his enlistment was up and he had to sign on for four more years or "at the convenience of the government." This latter choice meant he stayed until the war ended and usually meant no promotions. As a regular Marine (as opposed to a reserve Marine), a man like Iggy could expect at least another stripe or two during a four-year enlistment period. Sergeant Ignatovich was anxious to go home, but was troubled over which way he should remain a Marine.

To assist Iggy in his dilemma, I pointed out the war

would last at least two years. Then, the policing and usual bureaucratic fumbling another two year would be expended. I told Iggy I felt he should sign up for the four year hitch. Iggy thanked me for my good reasoning. Iggy signed on for four more years. The Atomic bomb dropped, peace was signed, the war was over. Ignatovich was looking for Private Peterson. Well, you can't win them all.

When Sergeant Ignatovich caught up with me, he was very rational. I told him with his war record, he should consider staying in the Corps until retirement. I had a distinct feeling Iggy wasn't weighing my advice as he had before.

While in the Marines everything seemed to move slow except bad news. The exception to the rule was the end of the war. We read of a new super bomb had been dropped on Japan. Later in the day it was called an atomic bomb. The newspapers said a whole city had been destroyed. Then in a few days another bomb had destroyed a second city. Then in just a few days we were at peace.

I had been contemplating leaving Miami on my way back to the Pacific (My four months were nearly up.) Now there was no need for Private Peterson. We were told of a point system for discharge. My overseas time and combat experiences gave me twice the required points for discharge. I was going home! I made it! Life is beautiful.

VJ Day (Victory - Japan) was celebrated everywhere. Unfortunately, I was on duty VJ day and had to limit my celebration to the base. As sailors and Marines staggered in, we poured them into jeeps and trucks and hauled them to their beds. There was no punishment for the revelers. We loved everybody. We got our share of kisses and hugs from celebrating Waves.

COUNTERING THE HOLLYWOOD CONCEPT OF THE ENLISTED SERVICEMAN

The Marines I served with in WWII were all high school graduates and many had attended college. We had our loudmouth braggards and quiet types on the same ratio one finds among civilians.

We were not a group of hard drinking louts. Although, while on liberty, we enjoyed the fruit of the vine, but not any more or less than our civilian counterparts. We flirted with girls, but were not heavy-handed lotharios.

We were a reflection of our civilian background and because of our great numbers, we were a genuine cross-section of young men of the United States in the 1940's.

I write this defense to counter the "dese," "dems," and "dose" characters so apparent in film versions of "our boys in the service" in World War II. Perhaps, this oafish type existed elsewhere, but the soldiers and sailors I met were in the main well-behaved and fairly well-read.

GOODBYE TO MARINE - OPA LOCKA

My last goodbyes to my fellow Marines at Opa Locka was a joyous sadness. Sergeant Moore expressed the opinion I should stay in the Marines. Sergeant Ignatovich expressed his fear my advice would no longer be available. Hyer said he'd miss me. (He had a year to go on his enlistment.) We all expressed a hope we would meet again some day. (We never have.)

Then we boarded the bus for downtown Miami. We were civilians. We were no longer active Marines. Our life was now our own. The freedom was intoxicating.

THE CIVILIAN

I sat in a restaurant in downtown Miami saying goodbye to Barbara Schultz. We couldn't believe I was discharged and was going home. It was hard to believe I was no longer in the Marine Corps. Barbara teared up as we walked to the Flagler Avenue train station. She thought she would be in the Spars until January 1946. I was discharged October 24, 1945.

My homecoming was all I expected it to be. The big

question was, "what now?" The only sensible answer was school. But where, had to be answered.

Jack O'Keefe came home Christmas of 1945 to a gala Christmas party at his house. All our returning friends showed up.

THE BEGINNING

After the Marines, I felt driven to continue my education. I spent a year at Drake University (1946-1947) with a lot of veteran friends. Then finished at the University of Michigan. On the University of Michigan campus, I ran into Major Verne Kennedy. He was surprised to see me. Oh yes, he asked me if I had waved at any Japanese tanks lately. He insisted I join his fraternity, Sigma Chi. We lived together in the attic of the Sigma Chi house for my first year at Michigan. Kennedy and others often asked me why I opted for schooling after the service. My stock answer was I had spent enough of my life as a Private even as lofty as a Private First Class. There had to be something after PFC.

LIFE AFTER THE WAR

I am pleased to announce the boys of the 12th Marine did well in their peace time pursuits.

Captain Moss became an executive with Lockheed Aeronautical Company.

Lt. Charles Presser returned to his family farm and nursery in Indiana after serving a stint in China after the war.

Bob Wolfe became a builder in Annapolis, Maryland and presently resides in an estate overlooking the United States Naval Academy.

Jack Kerins owned a sporting goods store in Terre Haute, Indiana and was a contributing writer for fishing and hunting publications.

Harry Yourell became a State Representative in Illinois.

John Saylor returned to house building in Arkansas.

Frank Seppi became a funeral director in upstate New York (Yes, even after swearing he'd never do it when he and Mayo were tapped for burial detail on Guam.)

Dan Devey became head of a heavy equipment company in Salt Lake City.

Lt. Colonel Fairborn became a Major General and commanded the 1st Marine Division.

Alvin Josephy continued his writing and is considered an expert on American Indians.

Harold Match returned to the Tulsa Telephone Company.

Dr. Peter Paulo returned to his practice in Mississippi.

Bob Applebaum served with the Marine Corps for 30 years.

Lou Hum worked for the US Post Office in California.

Jack Cross was with the United Airlines.

John Skutel runs his business in Connecticut. He's a dealer in books and maps.

I conclude this list apologizing to those not mentioned. This was caused by my not knowing what business or profession they entered. I do know everyone did us proud in their post-war pursuits and certainly married well.

PFC Eugene H. Peterson, 425802 served as a National Vice President of the American Cancer Society.

I DIDN'T KNOW THAT

Many years after graduating from University of Michigan, I sent an early edition of this book to a friend in Ann Arbor, Michigan. He, in turn, shared it with Richard Hadler, a fraternity brother from my school days.

Richard called me and expressed surprise that I had been a combat Marine in WWII. He had thought I was a V-12 student. (V-12 was an officer's training program at many colleges during WWII.) He then revealed he had been a combat Marine during the war in the 2nd Marine Division having fought at Tarawa and Saipan. He also told me another of our fraternity brothers, Denny Youngblood, had received the Navy Cross for heroic efforts on Saipan.

I expressed my surprise at his revelations and told him we obviously didn't talk much about our war time experiences after the war.

I am still amazed that I lived with Richard Hadler and Danny Youngblood for three years while we were students and never once touched on our WWII experiences.

One last Jack O'Keefe story: in the late 40's, I was working and living one summer in Chicago. I received a phone call about 2 am from Jack. He related he had just pulled the most dangerous stunt in two world wars. He continued he was at Higgins Bar in a tough area of South Chicago and didn't have enough to pay his bar tab. After I bailed him out of an eight dollar bar bill, I asked him how it had happened. He said he bought the house a round of drinks. I countered, "You bought the house a round of drinks when you were broke?" Jack simply replied, "It seemed to be the thing to do at the time." Jack, you are missed.

AFTERGLOW

After my discharge form the Armed Forces, I was fortunate on several occasions to have chance meetings with former Marine buddies.

In the body of this report, I have mentioned meeting Major Verne Kennedy on the University of Michigan campus.

THEN THERE WAS HERRON

During a summer break from the University, I traveled to Hannibal, Missouri and was seated on the porch of a local hotel. A young man approached me and challenged, "You're Peterson. We were in the Marines." I was startled but immediately recognized Herron, a former Corporal in the 12th Marines. He and I spent a pleasant evening recalling our days in the Corps.

MEETING CORPORAL KRAFT

Only a week after this surprise meeting with Herron, I was hitch-hiking in Iowa. As night overtook me, I found myself stranded in a tough Des Moines neighborhood. The cool summer evening unexpectedly became a wet summer evening. Seeking shelter from the downpour, I opted for a beer joint across the street.

I ordered a bottle of beer (20 cents) as payment for a few moments of shelter. (20 cents out of my total bank roll of 35 cents, hurt!)

As I reached for the bottle, the bartender placed his hand over the bottle top. This caused me to look at my aggressor. I was greeted with a broad smile. "I know you. We were in the Marines!" I responded, "My God, Kraft. I never could forget your ugly face."

He laughed and I told him I was in need of a friendly face.

We then entered into our past Marine Corps experiences and many "do you remember" stories, as he pushed back my 20 cents.

Kraft had placed his hand over my beer bottle for a purpose. Iowa law only permitted "near beer" (low alcohol content.) In many bars, if you were known, the bartender would fill the top of your beer bottle with grain alcohol or vodka, making it a potent beer.

Kraft, upon recognizing me, wanted to be sure I received the best he could provide.

After Kraft learned of my plight, we spent the night in the barroom. He offered me the largest booth and he slept in another booth. The next morning, he waited with me until I secured a ride out of Des Moines.

I made an effort to contact Kraft at a later date, but was told he had moved to the West Coast.

MY ACHING BACK

In 1952 I learned I had two vertebrae in my back that were crushed together and fused. The attending physician asked me when this could have happened. I recalled the pain I experienced when jumping into shallow water from the amphibious tractor on the Guam landing.

The physician said the pain must have been bad. I agreed but told the physician I could not bring myself to complain about a back ache with men dying and injured by enemy fire all around me. He agreed this would not have impressed even a sympathetic Sergeant.

AL MILLER REVISITED

On one of my many trips to Chicago during summer breaks from school, my dad asked me to pick up two hundred-pound bags of potatoes for our restaurant. I purchased these at the South State Street Wholesale Market.

When I entered the office to pay for my produce, I was surprised to find my old pal Al Miller from my days in M Battery, 12th Marines. I had last seen Al as I climbed aboard the ship that took us off Iwo Jima

I asked Al how life was treating him. We laughed in agreement over his response, "Anything is better than Iwo!"

Al said his father-in-law was ready to pay off his promise of a big night at the Chez Paris because I brought Al back to Chicago after the war.

I've tried to locate Al Miller but haven't been able to find him.

We have a saying in the Marine Corps: "Once a Marine, always a Marine."

I have found this to be very true.

IT COULD HAVE HAPPENED TO ME

At wars end, we heard about Colonels, Majors, and Captains being demoted back to their "permanent rank." Some even became Sergeants after having held temporary commissions. I always felt I left just in time. I do not believe I could stand to be broken back to a Buck Private. When one has soared to the heights, it is hard to fall back.

EPILOGUE

In 1994 I was invited back to Guam for the 50th celebration of this island's liberation. I was accompanied by a number of the Marines I had served with during this invasion and subsequent liberation.

These worthies were: Harold Match, Jack Kerins, Bill Arend, Bob Wolfe, Ed Jewsbury, and John McClure. Most of us had our spouses along.

The citizens of Guam were very effusive in their display of appreciation. We were given "Liberator" hats and the islanders would accost us in the hotel, on the streets or at the special event to tell us how much they appreciated what we had done for them, their family or relatives. At the Guam airport, we were welcomed by the Governor of Guam, the National representative to Congress, the Admiral of the Pacific Fleet, General of the Army

Pacific Command, and the Commandant of the Marine Corps. We were feted royally at many meetings and banquets. The Navy prepared a banquet and review aboard the Aircraft Carrier "Belleau Wood." We were honored royally.

We returned to Asan Beach where we had landed 50 years ago. A large monument was dedicated to those forces involved in the liberation.

We had the opportunity to revisit area where we had camped. There were no vestiges of our camp at Ylig bay. The area was overgrown and a private residence now sits in the place of our former camp.

I enjoyed being able to show Harold Match where he was hit by the mortar that sent him home. I joked about Match only lasting half hour in the Guam campaign.

The cemetery of Asan Beach was gone. All the fallen Marines' remains had either been sent to their home town or to the large service-cemetery in Hawaii (This was a choice given to the relatives of the fallen.)

The high point of the entire trip to Guam came at the Liberation Day Parade. Although already mentioned in the body of my report, it bears repeating. Twenty-five or thirty rain-drenched children stood before our reviewing stand and sang:

Oh Mr. Sam, Sam my dear old Uncle Sam

We are so glad you came back to Guam

We all fought back tears at this deeply-felt appreciative-expression for our long ago efforts.

Never a paragon of sensitivity, my son, Army Captain Mark Peterson wrote a parody to express his appreciation of my efforts on Guam;

> *Oh Peterson, Son, my dear old Peterson*
> *Won't you please come back to Guam*
> *Laying up the wire, climbing up the trees*
> *Three years Marine Corps, Still a PFC*

This also moved me to tears, and gave me the title for this book!

Our 12th Marine Headquarters and Service personnel still meet annually. At these meetings, we have Captain Moss, Lt. Charlie Presser (our Sergeant who was commissioned in the Field on Guam,) Bob Wolfe, Jack Kerins, Bill Arend, Frank Maio, Vic Lukas, Dick Hannon, Mike Heinzmann, CD Brown, John McClure, John Saylor, John Wardlow and Harold Match. These attend regularly and we have other who attend infrequently.

I still see Lou Hum of M Battery when I attend 3rd Marine Division reunions. Unfortunately Harold "Mayor" Kelly has not been heard from for many years.

We do not know if he is still living. George Cooper, my foxhole partner on Iwo Jima, is dead. I saw Al Miller in Chicago in the early 50's, but haven't heard from him or seen him since.

I attended Jack O'Keefe's funeral in Florida twenty years ago. It was the last time I saw his family.

LEST WE FORGET

TO ALL THOSE WHO DID NOT GET HOME
BUT DIED FOR US AND OUR WAY OF LIFE,

I SALUTE YOU

AS DOES YOUR COUNTRY.

BIBLIOGRAPHY

All photos cited are public domain unless otherwise stated.

"Bougainville USMC Photo No. 1-1." Flickr,https://www.flickr.com/photos/usmcarchives/21412034078/. Accessed 4 Dec. 2018.

"Bougainville USMC Photo No. 1-2." Flickr,https://www.flickr.com/photos/usmcarchives/21608738511/. Accessed 4 Dec. 2018.

"Bougainville USMC Photo No. 1-3." Flickr,https://www.flickr.com/photos/usmcarchives/21412937389/. Accessed 4 Dec. 2018.

"Bougainville USMC Photo No. 1-4." Flickr,https://www.flickr.com/photos/usmcarchives/21411828860/. Accessed 4 Dec. 2018.

"Bougainville USMC Photo No. 1-5." Flickr,https://www.flickr.com/photos/usmcarchives/21599939995/. Accessed 4 Dec. 2018.

"Bougainville USMC Photo No. 1-6." Flickr,https://www.flickr.com/photos/usmcarchives/21411827490/. Accessed 4 Dec. 2018.

"Bougainville USMC Photo No. 1-12." Flickr,https://www.flickr.com/photos/usmcarchives/21412037678/. Accessed 4 Dec. 2018.

"Bougainville USMC Photo No. 1-13." Flickr,https://www.flickr.com/photos/usmcarchives/21599940665/. Accessed 4 Dec. 2018.

"Bougainville USMC Photo No. 1-14." Flickr,https://www.flickr.com/photos/usmcarchives/20978746553/. Accessed 4 Dec. 2018.

"Bougainville USMC Photo No. 1-15." Flickr,https://www.flickr.com/photos/usmcarchives/21573683776/. Accessed 4 Dec. 2018.

"Bougainville USMC Photo No. 1-19." Flickr,https://www.flickr.com/photos/usmcarchives/21412032408/. Accessed 4 Dec. 2018.

*File:24th Marines Wwii Iwo Jima.jpg - Wikipedia.*https://en.wikipedia.org/wiki/File:24th_marines_wwii_iwo_jima.jpg. Accessed 4 Dec. 2018.

*File:37mm Gun Fires against Cave Positions at Iwo Jima.jpg - Wikipedia.*https://en.wikipedia.org/wiki/File: 37mm_Gun_fires_against_cave_positions_at_Iwo_Jima.j pg. Accessed 4 Dec. 2018.

*File:American Supplies Being Landed at Iwo Jima.JPEG - Wikipedia.*https://en.wikipedia.org/wiki/File: American_supplies_being_landed_at_Iwo_Jima.JPEG. Accessed 4 Dec. 2018.

*File:Browning M1917 Marine Iwo Jima Fixed.jpg - Wikipedia.*https://en.wikipedia.org/wiki/File: Browning_M1917_Marine_Iwo_Jima_fixed.jpg. Accessed 4 Dec. 2018.

*File:Captured Japanese Flag on Iwo Jima.jpg - Wikipedia.*https://en.wikipedia.org/wiki/File: Captured_Japanese_flag_on_Iwo_Jima.jpg. Accessed 4 Dec. 2018.

*File: Marine Receives Water.jpg - Daily Mail.*https://www. dailymail.co.uk/news/article-4777734/Harrowing-WWII-photos-brutal-battle-liberate-Guam.html

*File:Coast Guard Marines at Guam - Ca. July 1944.jpg - Wikipedia.*https://en.wikipedia.org/wiki/File: Coast_Guard_Marines_at_Guam_-_ca._July_1944.jpg. Accessed 4 Dec. 2018.

*File:First Flag on Guam - 1944.jpg - Wikipedia.*https://en.

wikipedia.org/wiki/File:First_flag_on_Guam_-
_1944.jpg. Accessed 4 Dec. 2018.

File:GuadLandingsLunga.jpg - *Wikipedia.*https://en.
wikipedia.org/wiki/File:GuadLandingsLunga.jpg.
Accessed 4 Dec. 2018.

File:Iwo Jima - Landing Plan.jpg - *Wikipedia.*https://en.
wikipedia.org/wiki/File:Iwo_Jima_-_Landing_Plan.jpg.
Accessed 4 Dec. 2018.

File:Iwo Jima Tunnels.JPG - *Wikipedia.*https://en.
wikipedia.org/wiki/File:Iwo_Jima_Tunnels.JPG.
Accessed 4 Dec. 2018.

*File:Marines Burrow in the Volcanic Sand on the Beach of Iwo
Jima.jpg* - *Wikipedia.*https://en.wikipedia.org/wiki/File:
Marines_burrow_in_the_volcanic_sand_on_the_beach_
of_Iwo_Jima.jpg. Accessed 4 Dec. 2018.

File:Marines Rest in the Field on Guadalcanal.jpg -
*Wikipedia.*https://en.wikipedia.org/wiki/File:
Marines_rest_in_the_field_on_Guadalcanal.jpg.
Accessed 4 Dec. 2018.

File:Marines with LVT(A)-5 in Iwo Jima 1945.jpg -
*Wikipedia.*https://en.wikipedia.org/wiki/File:
Marines_with_LVT(A)-5_in_Iwo_Jima_1945.jpg.
Accessed 4 Dec. 2018.

File:Ronson Flame Tank Iwo Jima.jpg - *Wikipedia.*https://en.
wikipedia.org/wiki/File:

Ronson_flame_tank_Iwo_Jima.jpg. Accessed 4 Dec. 2018.

*File:Stars and Stripes on Mount Suribachi (Iwo Jima).jpg - Wikipedia.*https://en.wikipedia.org/wiki/File: Stars_and_Stripes_on_Mount_Suribachi_(Iwo_Jima).jpg. Accessed 4 Dec. 2018.

*File:Three Marines and Their Machine Gun on Guam.jpg - Wikipedia.*https://en.wikipedia.org/wiki/File: Three_Marines_and_their_machine_gun_on_Guam.jpg. Accessed 4 Dec. 2018.

*File:Tracked Landing Vehicles (LVTs) Approach Iwo Jima;fig14.jpg - Wikipedia.*https://en.wikipedia.org/wiki/ File: Tracked_landing_vehicles_(LVTs)_approach_Iwo_Jima;f ig14.jpg. Accessed 4 Dec. 2018.

*File:US Marine Corps 155mm Rifle on White Beach, Guam.jpg - Wikipedia.*https://en.wikipedia.org/wiki/File: US_Marine_Corps_155mm_rifle_on_White_Beach,_G uam.jpg. Accessed 4 Dec. 2018.

*File:USMC-17446.jpg - Wikipedia.*https://en.wikipedia. org/wiki/File:USMC-17446.jpg. Accessed 4 Dec. 2018.

*File:USMC-M-Guam-OFC.jpg - Wikipedia.*https://en. wikipedia.org/wiki/File:USMC-M-Guam-OFC.jpg. Accessed 4 Dec. 2018.

"Marine Foxholes, Iwo Jima, 1945." Flickr,https://www.

flickr.com/photos/usmcarchives/35911122253/.
Accessed 4 Dec. 2018.

"Marine in Captured Anti-Aircraft Emplacement, Iwo
Jima, 1945." Flickr,https://www.flickr.com/photos/
usmcarchives/35885653714/. Accessed 4 Dec. 2018.

"Marines Pushing Jeep through Sand, Iwo Jima, 1945."
Flickr,https://www.flickr.com/photos/usmcarchives/
35885654674/. Accessed 4 Dec. 2018.

CPSIA information can be obtained
at www.ICGtesting.com
Printed in the USA
BVHW081702220721
612636BV00008B/439